P9-DEZ-814

Series/Number 07-093

REGRESSION WITH DUMMY VARIABLES

MELISSA A. HARDY
Florida State University

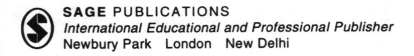

SAGE PUBLICATIONS
International Educational and Professional Publisher
Newbury Park   London   New Delhi

Copyright © 1993 by Sage Publications, Inc.

All rights reserved. No part of this book may be reproduced or utilized in any form or by any means, electronic or mechanical, including photocopying, recording, or by any information storage and retrieval system, without permission in writing from the publisher.

For information address:

SAGE Publications, Inc.
2455 Teller Road
Newbury Park, California 91320
E-mail: order@sagepub.com

SAGE Publications Ltd.
6 Bonhill Street
London EC2A 4PU
United Kingdom

SAGE Publications India Pvt. Ltd.
M-32 Market
Greater Kailash I
New Delhi 110 048 India

Printed in the United States of America

Hardy, Melissa A., 1952-
    Regression with dummy variables / Melissa A. Hardy.
        p.   cm.—(Qantitative applications in the social sciences;
    93)
    Includes bibliographical references.
    ISBN 978-0-8039-5128-0 (pbk.)
    1. Social sciences—Statistical methods.   2. Regression analysis.
    3. Dummy variables.   I.Title.   II. Series: Sage university papers
    series. Quantitative applications in the social sciences; 93.
    HA31.3.H37   1993
    300'.1'519536—dc20   92-41965

10 11 12 13 14 15   17 16 15 14 13 12

Sage Production Editor: Diane S. Foster

When citing a university paper, please use the proper form. Remember to cite the current Sage University Paper series title and include the paper number. One of the following formats can be adapted (depending on the style manual used):

(1) HARDY, M. A. (1993) Regression With Dummy Variables. Sage University Paper series on Quantitative Applications in the Social Sciences, 07-093. Newbury Park, CA: Sage.

OR

(2) Hardy, M. A. (1993). *Regression with dummy variables* (Sage University Paper series on Quantitative Applications in the Social Sciences, series no. 07-093). Newbury Park, CA: Sage.

CONTENTS

SERIES EDITOR'S INTRODUCTION

Upon first hearing the phrase *dummy variables,* beginning students of quantitative research methods often chuckle. However, they quickly learn the importance of dummy variables. Independent variables originally measured at the ordinal and nominal levels can make poor candidates for inclusion in a regression analysis. However, once they are "dummied up," ordinary least squares estimation goes forward without violating the level of measurement assumption.

What exactly is a dummy variable? Basically, it is a dichotomous variable constructed from an originally qualitative variable. The number of dichotomies one needs equals $G - 1$, where G is the number of original categories. For example, to represent the ordinal variable of citizens' political interest as measured in an opinion survey (three categories—*very, somewhat, not at all*), the researcher must construct two dichotomous variables. Say they are X_1 (scored 1 if *very,* 0 if otherwise) and X_2 (scored 1 if *somewhat,* 0 if otherwise). One observes that those respondents who score 0 on both X_1 and X_2 are necessarily *not at all* interested. Also, these *not at all* interested form a baseline, or reference, group from which to evaluate the regression coefficients of X_1 and X_2.

But why select *not at all* as the reference group rather than, say, *somewhat*? To such a question, and the many others dummy variable users face, Professor Hardy poses clear answers. Sticking with a well-conceived example on income determination, she moves from the simplest model—regression with one dummy variable (which reduces to a difference of means test)—to complex models with multiple dummies, quantitative variables, and interaction terms. Fortunately, the complexity is clarified by careful verbal explication of the meanings of the coefficients under the varying conditions.

After laying this firm foundation, Professor Hardy considers special problems of dummy variable regression. Among other things, she explains how to deal with heteroscedasticity, how to interpret coefficients when the dependent variable is logged or logit, how to make multiple comparisons in significance testing, how to carry out effects coding and contrast coding, how to test for curvilinearity, and how to conduct a piecewise linear regression.

In sum, Professor Hardy probes dummy variable usage from virtually every possible angle. No other writer on statistical methods offers anywhere near the coverage provided here. This accessibly written monograph, it seems safe to say, will be the definitive treatment of dummy variable regression for some time to come.

—*Michael S. Lewis-Beck*
Series Editor

REGRESSION WITH DUMMY VARIABLES

MELISSA A. HARDY
Florida State University

1. INTRODUCTION

Regression analysis is one of the most flexible and widely used techniques of quantitative analysis. A typical regression model attempts to explain variation in a quantitative dependent variable, Y_i, by mapping the relationship of Y to a specified set of independent variables as an additive, linear function. Using least squares estimation techniques, we arrive at a prediction equation that allows us to estimate conditional means on the dependent variable—expected values of Y for specific combinations of values on the independent variables. When the independent variables are measurable as quantitative variables for which we can assume roughly equal intervals relative to an arbitrary zero point, the number of possible predicted values for Y is unlimited. Further, when both dependent and independent variables are quantitative variables, the set of relationships can be captured geometrically.

In a bivariate regression in which we predict Y as a function of only one independent variable, the relationship between the two variables is captured by the regression line. All points along the line represent conditional mean values of Y. When a second independent variable is included in the specification, the one-dimensional line is extended to two dimensions, and we have a plane with a particular tilt in the north-south direction and a particular tilt in the east-west direction. All points on this plane also represent predicted mean values of Y for specific combinations of values on the two independent variables. As the number of independent variables increases, the principles remain the same even though the geometry may no longer be easily visualized.

But the usefulness of the regression model would be severely limited if all independent variables used as predictors had to be measured on an interval scale. Research questions involving group differences are quite common. For example, social scientists are often interested in

1

explaining racial/ethnic differences, gender differences, or regional differences in behavior, attitudes, or socioeconomic characteristics. Market researchers want to understand the demographics of consumer preferences. In addition, researchers frequently want to know whether the effects of independent variables are the same for all groups, or whether group differences in the strength or direction of a relationship also exist. Many research questions therefore seek to identify group differences in levels of a dependent variable as well as group differences in the effects of independent variables.

When independent variables of interest are qualitative (i.e., "measured" at only the nominal level), we require a technique that allows us to represent this information in quantitative terms without imposing unrealistic measurement assumptions on the categorical variables. For example, if occupational categories are coded from 1 through 12 (the categorization used in single-digit census codes), it is not reasonable simply to include occupation as a variable that ranges from a low value of 1 to a high value of 12, because this treatment assumes an underlying measurement scale of equal intervals. Defining a set of dummy variables allows us to capture the information contained in a categorization scheme and then to use this information in a standard regression estimation. In fact, the set of independent variables specified in a regression equation can include any combination of qualitative and quantitative predictors.

For example, the societal distribution of resources through earnings is a concern that is common to both academics interested in inequality and citizens trying to maintain their standard of living. Our beliefs about social justice are often based on perceptions of resource distribution and whether certain groups seem to be advantaged or disadvantaged in the distributive process. A common approach to studying discrimination in the distribution of earned income, for example, is to begin by identifying a group difference—a difference between women and men, or between blacks and whites—as the gross effect of being in the less privileged rather than the more privileged group, and then to investigate whether this gross difference is maintained after additional determinants of resource distribution are included in the specification. By using this technique, researchers try to identify the social process that has produced the observed inequality.

In order to provide continuity in the discussion of statistical technique, I will frequently invoke the substantive example of predicting earned income as a function of individual characteristics that can be captured by both qualitative and quantitative variables. Data are from the first wave of the National Longitudinal Surveys of Older Men. The respondents in the original sample are representative of approximately 15 million men in the U.S. civilian noninstitutionalized population who were ages 45 to 59 in 1966, the date of the first interview.[1] The independent variables of interest to us in this example will include race, occupation (U.S. Census classification), education (years of schooling), and job tenure (years with the same employer). Although other variables can be hypothesized as predictors of yearly income from wages and salary (e.g., labor supply, job skills, health), I will limit this exercise to just four predictors that provide us with a combination of quantitative and qualitative measures. By explicating the technique of regression with dummy variables through a discussion of progressively complex models predicting a single dependent variable, I will attempt to show clearly how the interpretation of the coefficient for any particular dummy variable is contingent on the overall specification of the model. I hope thereby to reduce the likelihood that readers will attempt to generalize interpretations to situations in which they are no longer appropriate.

The discussion will begin somewhat naively, with initial concern focused on differences in earnings income (measured in dollars per year) between blacks and whites. Then we will gradually build models that call into question a number of assumptions embedded in the earlier specifications. We will examine whether the group difference between average earnings for blacks and whites persists when we control for additional qualitative and quantitative independent variables. Then we will test whether the net effects of the independent variables are the same for blacks and whites. Ultimately, we will use the dummy variable regression format to estimate race-specific effects for all parameters in the regression model. This gradual process of unfolding increasingly complex specifications will take us through Chapter 4. Although the distribution of earned income may not be of equal interest to all readers, the types of measures used are straightforward and accessible to readers regardless of disciplinary background. Further, the types of interpretations appropriate to different model specifications are easily extended to any substantive issue. Chapter 5 provides a fairly brief description of alternative coding strategies for dummy variables. In Chapter 6, we move away from our single-problem focus to consider other types of research situations in which dummy variables can be useful.

A Review of Multiple Regression

The discussion that follows assumes that the reader is already familiar with single-equation regression models, the concept and technique of partialing, and hypothesis testing. Readers who are not comfortable with this material should turn first to introductory texts on regression. Earlier volumes in this series (e.g., Berry & Feldman, 1985; Lewis-Beck, 1980; Schroeder, Sjoquist, & Stephan, 1986), as well as basic statistics texts (e.g., Bohrnstedt & Knoke, 1982; Cohen & Cohen, 1983), provide useful discussions of these topics.

By way of establishing the notation that will be used in this text, however, we can review a few of the basics. Assume we have a quantitative dependent variable (Y_i), which we express as a linear function of three quantitative independent variables, X_{1i}, X_{2i}, and X_{3i}. The population regression function is

$$Y_i = \beta_0 + \beta_1 X_{1i} + \beta_2 X_{2i} + \beta_3 X_{3i} + u_i = \beta_0 + \sum \beta_k X_{ki} + u_i, \quad [1.1]$$

where k refers to the kth independent variable and i refers to the ith observation. This equation expresses Y_i as a linear additive function of the independent variables X_{1i}, X_{2i}, X_{3i} and the stochastic error term, u_i; β_0 is the intercept term (the value of Y_i when all independent variables are set to zero); β_1 is the population partial regression coefficient indicating the increment or decrement in the expected value of Y_i associated with a unit change in X_{1i}, controlling for the other independent variables in the equation; β_2 and β_3 are the comparable coefficients for X_{2i} and X_{3i}, respectively. The population regression function thereby provides the conditional means or expected values of Y_i for fixed values of X_{ki}. We rely on the sample regression function

$$Y_i = B_0 + B_1 X_{1i} + B_2 X_{2i} + B_3 X_{3i} + e_i \quad [1.2]$$

to produce least squares estimates of the population parameters. Each of the regression coefficients—B_0, B_1, B_2, and B_3—is a point estimator of the corresponding population parameter noted in Equation 1.1; it is also one observed value from the sampling distribution of the statistic. We use the observed values of e_i^2 to estimate the population variances and standard deviations of the sampling distributions (standard errors) of B_0, B_1, B_2, and B_3 so that we may evaluate the statistical significance

of our estimates and draw some conclusions about relationships between Y and X_k in the population. The standard error may also be used
to construct an interval estimator, called the confidence interval, which
is also useful in evaluating the strength or weakness of the statistical
evidence pertaining to hypotheses. Applying ordinary least squares
(OLS) analysis to these sample data is appropriate when we can accept
as reasonable the following assumptions:

1. $E(u_i|X_k) = 0$; that is, the mean value of u_i, conditional on given values of
   X_k, is zero.
2. $\text{cov}(u_i, u_j) = 0$; that is, the disturbances are independent for all $i \neq j$.
3. $\text{var}(u_i) = \sigma^2$; that is, the variance of u_i for each X_k value is equal to some
   positive constant, σ^2; this is also known as the assumption of homoscedasticity.
4. $\text{cov}(u_i, X_k) = 0$; the disturbances and explanatory variables are indepen-
   dently distributed.

Under these assumptions, OLS estimators are the best linear unbiased
estimators—"best" because they have the smallest variance in the class
of all linear unbiased estimators.

The problem of heteroscedasticity is usually associated with cross-
sectional data (data that describe units of a population at a given point
in time), whereas the problem of autocorrelation is more common with
time-series data (data that describe an entity over a period of time).
Dummy variables can prove useful in both cross-sectional and time-
series research. We can use dummy variables in cross-sectional research
to estimate differences between groups and to evaluate whether group
membership moderates the effects of other explanatory variables. Similarly, we can use dummy variables in time-series analysis to determine
whether one time period differs from a second time period and to test
for the stability of effects across time (Gujarati, 1970). Because dummy
variables are often used to define groups of observations in time-series
analysis as well as in cross-sectional analysis, the researcher must be
careful to address the issue of heteroscedasticity in both contexts. By
specifying dummy variables to capture group differences in cross-
sectional research, we acknowledge that information on potentially
heterogeneous groups has been pooled, or combined. If the error variances of these groups are significantly different—if we violate the assumption of homoscedasticity—the significance tests for individual coefficients
become unreliable. A similar problem characterizes time-series models

where dummy variables are used to test the stability of coefficients across two (or more) time periods. If the error variance differs significantly across the periods, the condition of heteroscedasticity makes inferential tests problematic (Maddala, 1992). Extensive discussions of the assumptions, the consequences of violating assumptions, and the types of remedial action most useful in dealing with assumption violations are available in most intermediate statistics texts. I will address these issues as they relate to the use of dummy variables and return to discussions of heteroscedasticity and autocorrelation later in the text.

We can evaluate the overall fit of the regression model to the sample data using R^2, which is the square of the multiple correlation coefficient. Tests of statistical significance for individual regression coefficients are accomplished through t tests. We use the t distribution rather than the Z distribution because we generally do not know the value of the population variance (σ^2); therefore we produce an estimate of the population variance using the error variance of the sample. When testing against a null hypothesis that the effect (or partial effect) is equal to zero, the t test reduces to the ratio of the coefficient estimate to its standard error.

Because three independent variables are included in the specification, B_1, B_2, and B_3 estimate the "partial" effects of X_1, X_2, and X_3 on Y. Partial effects are generally not equal to bivariate effects (when Y is regressed on only one independent variable) because independent variables included in a given specification are often correlated with each other and share covariation with Y_i. When the correlation between one independent variable (e.g., X_{1i}) and one or more remaining independent variables is perfect (i.e., when one independent variable is a perfect linear function of one or more of the other independent variables included in the specification), sample estimates are indeterminate. At an intuitive level, we can view the reason for this indeterminacy as a function of the absence of "unique" information: The information contained in the distribution of X_{1i} simply reproduces the statistical information already included on the right-hand side of the equation; it is impossible to estimate the net (i.e., partial or "unique") effect of X_{1i} on Y when X_{1i} provides no net (partial or unique) distributional information. This situation is referred to as *perfect multicollinearity*. Statistically, the reason for the indeterminacy can be understood by recalling exactly what we mean when we say other independent variables are "controlled" in the estimation of "partial" regression coefficients. To "hold constant" in a statistical sense requires that we remove from the

Y_i distribution all variability related to other independent variables in the model. Statistical "control" is therefore a procedure of partitioning variances. In our sample regression function (Equation 1.2), we remove from Y the linear effects of X_{2i} and X_{3i} when determining B_1. In other words, if X_{2i} and X_{3i} were not allowed to vary in our sample, we would not observe in the distribution of Y or in the distribution of X_{1i} that portion of variability that is associated with the variability of X_{2i} and X_{3i}. Therefore, in estimating the partial effect of X_{1i} on Y, we do not want that part of the variability in X_{1i} or Y to be considered. Essentially, then, the partial effect of X_{1i} on Y_i is based on two distributions of residuals—the residual distribution of Y_i after the linear effects of X_{2i} and X_{3i} have been removed from Y_i, and the residual distribution of X_{1i} after the linear effects of X_{2i} and X_{3i} have been subtracted from X_{1i}. In the case of perfect multicollinearity, this residual distribution of X_{1i} is a constant—zero.

When we include dummy variables in a regression equation, the logic of regression estimation remains the same: We are predicting conditional means on the dependent variable—that is, average values of Y given specific values on the independent variables. The difference is that specific codes on dummy variables designate membership in particular groups or the presence versus absence of particular characteristics. Therefore, predicting expected values of Y for a particular combination of dummy variable codes can be the same thing as predicting a group mean value. As is the case when the independent variables are continuous, this partialing procedure is also central to the interpretation of regression with dummy variables.

2. CREATING DUMMY VARIABLES

The coding of categorical data requires the development of mutually exclusive and exhaustive categories. The same rules apply to the creation of dummy variables. We need to construct a large enough set of dummy variables to exhaust the information contained in the original qualitative scale. Categorical variables can be dichotomous or polytomous. A categorical variable with j categories requires a set of $j - 1$ dummy variables in order to capture all the distributional information contained in the original set of distinctions. Using binary $(0,1)$ coding, dummy variables are always dichotomous variables. All respondents who are members of a particular category are assigned a code of 1;

respondents not in that particular category receive a code of 0. Following this coding convention, we construct a set of dummy variables for a given categorization so that any particular respondent is coded 1 on one and only one dummy variable in the set. The binary coding can be thought of as similar to an electrical switch: A code of 1 signals that a given category is "on" for a respondent (i.e., he or she is a member of that particular group, or a particular characteristic is present); for nonmembers, the dummy variable denoting that category is switched "off" (i.e., the characteristic is absent).

The rationale for including $j - 1$ dummy variables for a qualitative variable of j categories follows directly from the requirements of the classical linear regression model. In particular, the presumption of no perfect collinearity among independent variables requires that none of the explanatory variables can be written as a perfect linear combination of remaining explanatory variables in the model. Consider the dummy variable representing race in our example. If, in addition to a dummy variable (BLACK) coded 1 for a respondent who is African American, we include a second dummy variable (WHITE) coded 1 for a respondent who is not African American, we have specified a model in which a perfect linear relationship exists between the two independent variables, because

$$BLACK = 1 - WHITE.$$

Therefore, the information contained in WHITE is redundant and unnecessary to the estimation.

When the original variable has only two categories, as in the case of race in this analysis, a single dummy variable is sufficient to capture the information. The category not named as a dummy variable serves as the reference group. If the original variable has more than two categories, the number of dummy variables is governed by the number of separate categories one wishes to contrast in the analysis. By way of illustration, consider the variable occupation, as measured by the census coding of 12 single-digit occupational categories. In this example, we could have as many as 11 dummy variables, the twelfth category serving as our reference group. In order to make our illustrative analysis a bit more manageable, however, we will exclude farm managers and farm laborers and combine some of the remaining groups so that we consider only six separate categories: OCC_1 (upper white-collar workers—e.g., professionals, managers), OCC_2 (lower white-collar workers—clerks, salesmen), OCC_3 (skilled craftsmen—carpenters, plumbers, electricians), OCC_4 (operatives—welders, weavers, sewers, and stitchers in manufacturing), OCC_5 (nonhousehold service workers—barbers, janitors, practical nurses), and OCC_6 (laborers—fishermen, lumbermen, teamsters). Following the rule set forth above, a variable with six mutually exclusive and exhaustive categories requires five dummy variables to represent all the information contained in the original qualitative variable. Five of the categories will be represented by separate dummy variables; the sixth category (the "excluded" category, i.e., the category not named by one of the dummy variables) will serve as the reference group.

Choosing a Reference Group

Before we actually code the data for some number of categorical variables, we must choose our reference groups. Which groups do we want to serve as the comparison points? For each categorical variable, we must designate a single category as the reference group. In our example, if we choose "white" as the reference category, then the bivariate regression coefficient for the dummy variable BLACK will express the average income for African American men relative to the average income for white American men. In other words, the regression coefficient will express the difference between the two group means. If "white" is the reference group, then the bivariate regression coefficient, B, for the dummy variable BLACK is as follows:

$$B_{BLACK} = \overline{Y}_{BLACK} - \overline{Y}_{WHITE} .$$

In contrast, if African Americans serve as the reference group, then the bivariate regression coefficient, B', for the dummy variable WHITE is:

$$B'_{WHITE} = \overline{Y}_{WHITE} - \overline{Y}_{BLACK} .$$

Regardless of which category is chosen as the reference group, the absolute value of the difference in average income will be the same.

Choosing a reference group for a polytomous variable such as occupation is somewhat more involved. The regression coefficients for all occupational dummy variables will be evaluated relative to this single reference group. Although we can always use the information from any single regression estimation (with its particular specification regarding reference group) to generate additional comparisons, there are a few guidelines that may prove useful from the standpoint of interpreting regression estimates:

1. The reference group should be well defined. A residual category ("other") may not be a good choice, as it is unclear exactly what the composition of the "other" group is. It is also unlikely that the substantive interest in estimating group differences is reflected in comparisons of more homogeneous categories to this residual category. Therefore, by choosing a clearly defined group as reference point, we can explicitly build into the equation the group comparisons that are substantively important.

2. When there is an underlying ordinality to the qualitative categories (as in this case of occupation), some researchers choose as reference group a category at the upper or lower boundary, whereas others prefer to designate a category that is roughly midrange. Although the former approach may provide an array of coefficient estimates that can be interpreted relative to some anchor or ceiling group, the latter approach reduces the likelihood that less careful researchers will seize on one statistically significant coefficient (e.g., the contrast between laborers and upper white-collar workers) without first checking to see if occupation, as a multicategory predictor, registers a significant effect (this issue is discussed further at the end of Chapter 4).

3. A reference group should contain a sufficient number of cases to allow a reasonably precise estimate of the subgroup mean. Occasionally, one may define a separate category that contains only a small number of observations in an effort to keep other categories "pure." When this strategy is used, the reference category should be one of the more heavily populated categories.

Readers should keep in mind that, on statistical grounds, the choice of reference group is arbitrary; assuming one follows appropriate procedures of interpretation and inference, no choice can be "wrong." On practical grounds, the "best" choice is the one that minimizes the number of additional computations necessary to produce the information of most substantive interest.

Table 2.1 provides an illustration of the coding procedures just described. For the race variable, we choose white as the reference group; for occupation, we choose upper white-collar. African American respondents are coded 1 on BLACK and white respondents are coded 0. OCC_2, OCC_3, OCC_4, OCC_5, and OCC_6 are a set of five dummy variables designed to capture the information from the six-category

TABLE 2.1

Illustration of Dummy Variable Coding for Race and Occupation

Case	Race	Occupation	BLACK	OCC_2	OCC_3	OCC_4	OCC_5	OCC_6
1	black	lower white-collar	1	1	0	0	0	0
2	white	craftsman	0	0	1	0	0	0
3	white	upper white-collar	0	0	0	0	0	0
4	black	operative	1	0	0	1	0	0
5	black	laborer	1	0	0	0	0	1
6	white	lower white-collar	0	1	0	0	0	0
7	white	craftsman	0	0	1	0	0	0
8	white	service	0	0	0	0	1	0
9	black	service	1	0	0	0	1	0
10	white	upper white-collar	0	1	0	0	0	0
11	white	operative	0	0	0	1	0	0
12	white	lower white-collar	0	1	0	0	0	0
13	black	craftsman	1	0	1	0	0	0
14	white	upper white-collar	0	0	0	0	0	0
15	black	upper white-collar	1	0	0	0	0	0

occupational variable: OCC_2 refers to lower white-collar workers, OCC_3 to skilled craftsmen, OCC_4 to operatives, OCC_5 to service workers, and OCC_6 to laborers. Cases 3, 14, and 15 receive 0 codes on all five dummy variables because these three respondents were upper white-collar workers. In fact, Cases 3 and 14 receive 0 codes on all the dummy variables, because these two respondents are members of the reference categories for both qualitative variables: white and upper white-collar workers.

The qualitative information contained in the original race and occupation measures has thus been translated into information that can be used to calculate measures of central tendency, measures of dispersion, measures of correlation, and regression coefficients. An important feature of using $j - 1$ dummy variables rather than the original categorical variable lies in the fact that each dummy variable captures one piece of the categorical information from the original measure. For example, each dummy variable records the presence or absence of a single occupational characteristic (e.g., 1 if the characteristic of being a laborer is present, 0 if that characteristic is absent). We have not fundamentally altered the content of the information contained in either the race or occupation variables, we have only chosen an alternative form of representing that information. Therefore, so long as we adjust our interpretation of regression coefficients to be consistent with the underlying measurement properties of our independent variables, we are on solid statistical ground.

Descriptive Statistics

DISTRIBUTIONAL STATISTICS

Because dummy variables refer to qualitative measures, descriptive information on category frequencies or proportions is a useful way to display the distributions. Two of the most common measures of central tendency—the mode and the mean—can yield useful information as well.

The mean value of a dummy variable reports the proportion of cases in the category coded 1. Recall that a proportion is simply a relative frequency—a count of the number of cases in a given category divided by the total number of cases (i.e., n_j/N). Recall also that the formula for a mean value requires that the value of the measure be summed across all cases and then divided by the number of cases. Given that all cases are coded either 0 or 1 on a dummy variable, summing values across all cases is equivalent to counting the number of cases coded 1. Therefore, the formulas for a proportion and for the mean are equivalent in the case of dummy variables.

Likewise, the formula for the variance of a dummy variable can be related to the more general variance formula for continuous measures:

$$(\sum X_i^2)/N - (\sum X_i/N)^2 = n_j/N - p_j^2 = p_j - p_j^2 = p_j(1 - p_j). \quad [2.1]$$

When X_i is continuous, the variance formula is defined by the expression to the left of the first equal sign. When applying the same formula to a dummy variable, the term $\sum X_i^2$ reduces to n_j, the number of cases coded 1. Having already established that the term immediately to the left of the first equal sign, the mean squared, is equivalent to the square of the proportion of cases coded 1 for a dummy variable, we demonstrate that the variance for a dummy variable is the product of the proportion of cases coded 1 and its complement (the proportion of cases coded 0).

Variability in a dummy variable is maximized when cases are evenly split between the two categories. Think about a public opinion question: Do you support increasing taxes for public education? Maximum diversity—in this case, maximum disagreement over tax policy—occurs when people are evenly divided on the issue; the probability of choosing at random two members of the population who agree on the issue is at its lowest point. As we move toward consensus (as the percentage of respondents indicating support or opposition approaches 100), diversity of opinion (or variability) declines.

CORRELATION

In addition to measures that summarize the distributions of single variables, researchers are also interested in measures of association that summarize the relationship between variables. Typically we investigate the relationship between qualitative variables through cross-tabular analysis, and we assess the relationship between qualitative and quantitative measures by examining differences in means across categories of the discrete variable. Limiting ourselves initially to three measures, we can look at differences in mean income by occupation and race, as in the example shown in Table 2.2.

Three basic patterns are apparent in these descriptive statistics:

1. Blacks have a lower mean income than whites.
2. Mean income declines as we move from upper white-collar workers to laborers.
3. The proportion of workers who are black increases as we move from the upper white-collar to the laborer category.

Now we must develop ways to summarize the three bivariate relationships, test their significance, and extend our ability to assess relationships while controlling for additional relevant factors.

Given that both the mean and the variance of a dummy variable are linked to p_j, relational measures that are based on sample variances and covariances will also be linked to the proportional distribution of the dummy variable. A common measure of association is the correlation coefficient, a measure based on the covariance between two variables relative to the dispersion of their distributions. The correlation between two quantitative measures is sensitive to the amount of variance in the original distributions. Because the variance of a dummy variable is a direct function of p_j, the magnitude of a correlation involving a dummy variable will reflect the relative size of the category frequencies.

Table 2.3 contains estimated zero-order correlation coefficients for the dummy variables constructed from race and occupation and the

TABLE 2.2

Means and Standard Deviations of Income by Race, Occupation;
Occupation by Race

	Mean Income	Percentage Black
Race		
white	7,821.9	
($N = 2,290$)	(4,974.8)	
black	4,619.0	
($N = 921$)	(2,428.1)	
Occupation		
upper white-collar (OCC_1)	10,702.1	6.8
($N = 644$)	(7,166.5)	
whites	10,960.3	
($N = 602$)	(7,273.2)	
blacks	7,001.8	
($N = 42$)	(3,874.5)	
lower white-collar (OCC_2)	7,680.9	17.1
($N = 337$)	(4,228.7)	
whites	8,061.3	
($N = 279$)	(4,462.6)	
blacks	5,850.8	
($N = 58$)	(2,039.9)	
skilled (OCC_3)	6,945.0	17.7
($N = 810$)	(2,864.9)	
whites	7,334.7	
($N = 665$)	(2,786.9)	
blacks	5,157.8	
($N = 145$)	(2,526.0)	
operative (OCC_4)	5,553.9	38.9
($N = 788$)	(2,454.1)	
whites	6,085.3	
($N = 481$)	(2,414.6)	
blacks	4,721.4	
($N = 307$)	(2,281.5)	
service (OCC_5)	4,434.4	51.2
($N = 287$)	(2,352.0)	
whites	4,805.6	
($N = 139$)	(2,626.5)	
blacks	4,085.8	
($N = 148$)	(2,008.3)	
laborer (OCC_6)	4,090.0	64.0
($N = 345$)	(2,020.1)	
whites	4,777.3	
($N = 124$)	(1,900.1)	
blacks	3,704.3	
($N = 221$)	(1,986.6)	

TABLE 2.3
Correlation Coefficients: Race, Occupation, and Income

	Low White-Collar (OCC2)	Skilled (OCC3)	Operative (OCC4)	Service (OCC5)	Laborer (OCC6)	INCOME
BLACK	-.087***	-.139***	.131***	.157***	.272***	-.313***
OCC2 (low white-collar)		-.199***	-.196***	-.108***	-.119***	.057***
OCC3 (skilled)			-.328***	-.181***	-.199***	.007
OCC4 (operative)				-.178***	-.197***	-.166***
OCC5 (service)					-.108***	-.170***
OCC6 (laborer)						-.211***
Mean	.106	.250	.244	.089	.107	6,890
s.d.	.308	.433	.430	.285	.309	4,622

NOTE: ***Coefficient is statistically significant at the .001 level.

dependent variable, earned income. The far right column reports correlations (point biserial correlation coefficients) between each dummy variable and INCOME. The first value (-.313) summarizes the relationship between the dummy variable BLACK and INCOME. The negative sign indicates that the higher code on BLACK (coded 1 if African American) is associated with smaller values on INCOME; in other words, the mean value of INCOME among African-American men is lower than the mean INCOME for other men. By squaring the correlation coefficient, we calculate the proportion of the sample variance in INCOME that is "explained" by race. In this case, almost 10% of the variance in income is accounted for by the group difference in mean income.

Because more than one dummy variable was necessary to capture the information in the classification of occupations, we have five correlation coefficients describing the relationship between OCCUPATION and INCOME—one for each specified occupational category. Each of these five zero-order correlation coefficients assesses the income differential between the designated category (e.g., service workers in the case of OCC5) and all other workers combined. For example, the correlation between OCC5 and INCOME is -.170, indicating that service workers average lower incomes than all other workers taken together (i.e., upper white-collar, lower white-collar, skilled, operatives, and laborers combined as a single group). By squaring the zero-order correlation coefficient, we estimate how much of the variation in INCOME is due to the fact that men in one occupational group earn more or less than men who are not in that group. Here, 2.89% of the variance in INCOME is due to the fact that service workers average lower earnings than all other categories of workers taken together. Note also that the correlation between OCC_3 (skilled workers versus all others) and INCOME is small and nonsignificant. From this measure we learn that the average income of skilled workers is not significantly different from the mean income for all other categories of workers combined, a finding consistent with the intermediate position of skilled workers in both the occupation and income distributions.

Remaining columns of correlations refer to the association between two dummy variables taken two at a time. Correlations among two dummy variables are equivalent to phi (φ) coefficients and therefore are related to χ^2, because $\varphi = (\chi^2/N)^{1/2}$. Both measures capture the relationship between measures in a 2×2 table. The first row contains correlations between BLACK and each of the dummy variables constructed from OCCUPATION. The negative correlation between OCC_2 and BLACK suggests that the proportion of blacks in lower white-collar positions is smaller than the proportion of blacks in other occupational categories. On the other hand, the positive correlation coefficients between BLACK and OCC_4, OCC_5, and OCC_6 indicate that the proportion of blacks who are operatives (38.9%), service workers (57.2%), or laborers (64.0%) is greater than the proportion who are not operatives (25.1%), not service workers (26.3%), or not laborers (24.3%). The correlation is strongest between BLACK and OCC_6 (laborers) because the difference in proportions between the two categories is largest here.[2]

PARTIAL CORRELATIONS

Partial correlation coefficients allow us to assess the relationship between a dependent variable and an independent variable while other independent variables are held constant. Table 2.4 reports a series of partial correlation coefficients between OCC_2 (lower white-collar) and INCOME (Y) as successive controls are introduced.

Whereas the zero-order correlation between OCC_2 and INCOME simply contrasts average income for lower white-collar workers to all other workers, the first-order partial correlation coefficient, $r_{y,occ2.occ3}$,

TABLE 2.4

Partial and Semipartial Correlation Coefficients for
Occupation Dummies and Income

	Partial	Semipartial	Semipartial^2
$r_{y,occ2}$	$= .057$***		
$r_{y,occ2.occ3}$	$= .060$***		
$r_{y,occ2.occ3,occ4}$	$= .011$		
$r_{y,occ2.occ3,occ4,occ5}$	$= -.068$***		
$r_{y,occ2.occ3,occ4,occ5,occ6}$	$= -.171$***		
$r_{y,occ2.occ3,occ4,occ5,occ6}$	$-.171$***	$-.191$***	.036
$r_{y,occ3.occ2,occ4,occ5,occ6}$	$-.271$***	$-.294$***	.087
$r_{y,occ4.occ2,occ3,occ5,occ6}$	$-.369$***	$-.387$***	.150
$r_{y,occ5.occ2,occ3,occ4,occ6}$	$-.337$***	$-.357$***	.127
$r_{y,occ6.occ2,occ3,occ4,occ5}$	$-.378$***	$-.394$***	.155

NOTE: ***Coefficient is statistically significant at the .001 level.

controls for the craftsmen category. Because craftsmen are now held to the side, this partial correlation captures in correlational terms the income differential between lower white-collar workers and workers who are neither lower white-collar workers nor craftsmen. The next coefficient is a second-order partial correlation coefficient, because it controls for two independent variables (OCC_3 and OCC_4, the skilled and operative categories). In this example, the nonsignificance of the coefficient suggests that average income for lower white-collar workers is not significantly different from the average income of upper white-collar workers, laborers, and service workers combined—no doubt because this combination of high- and low-income groups results in a midrange mean value. As additional occupational categories are held constant—that is, excluded from the comparison—the higher order partials become increasingly negative. The highest or fourth-order partial controls for all other included occupational categories; it indicates that lower white-collar workers average significantly lower incomes than upper white-collar workers—the reference group, which is the only remaining group because all other included groups are controlled.

The lower panel of Table 2.4 provides fourth-order partial correlation coefficients for all occupational dummy variables. In each case, the partial captures the relationship between INCOME and a dichotomy represented by the specified occupational category and upper white-collar workers (the reference group). The negative values of the partials increase as we move down the column because the magnitude of the income difference is greatest when laborers are compared with upper white-collar workers and smallest when categories of white-collar workers are compared.

The middle and right columns of Table 2.4 report values for the semipartial and squared semipartial correlation coefficients. Semipartial correlation coefficients are useful bridges between correlation and regression. The partialing procedure used in the construction of partial correlation coefficients is the same as that used in the construction of partial regression coefficients; it affects the distributions of both the dependent and the independent variables. However, with semipartial correlation coefficients, the effects of independent variables that are being controlled are not partialed from the dependent variable (Cohen & Cohen, 1983). The square of the semipartial correlation coefficient indicates an independent variable's unique contribution to explained variance in Y_i, where "unique" explained variance is defined as that portion of the variance in Y_i that is attributable to one independent variable and not shared with other independent variables serving as controls. For example, the first squared semipartial correlation coefficient between INCOME and OCC_2, controlling for OCC_3, OCC_4, OCC_5, and OCC_6, is .036. By defining lower white-collar workers as a category distinct from upper white-collar workers, we account for 3.6% of the variance in INCOME. In other words, 3.6% of the variance in INCOME is explained by the fact that lower white-collar workers average a different level of earnings from upper white-collar workers. Similarly, 15.5% of the variance in INCOME can be explained by specifying the earnings differential between laborers and upper white-collar workers. Other factors equal, the more disparate the group values, the larger the amount of explained variance we sacrifice by ignoring the group difference.[3]

3. USING DUMMY VARIABLES AS REGRESSORS

In this chapter we will explore four regression models with dummy variables. The simplest model expresses the dependent variable, earned income, as a linear function of a single dummy variable. The second model is similar to the first in that it expresses income as a linear function of a single explanatory characteristic—in this case, occupation rather than race; however, because occupation is polytomous, the regression specification requires five dummy variables. In the third model, we include both qualitative variables to determine whether racial differences in income can be located in race-linked differences in occupational distributions. In the last model in this chapter, we expand the specification to include quantitative explanatory variables in addition to the dummy variables for occupation and race.

In estimating a bivariate regression equation, we determine whether the expected value of the dependent variable differs in a systematic way for given values of the independent variable. The regression equation therefore extends the mean from a single point representing the expected value of the dependent variable, $E(Y_i)$, to a line constructed from a continuous series of values. Each point on the line estimates the expected value of Y_i conditional on a particular value of X_{ki}, denoted $E(Y_i|X_{ki})$. The continuity in this series of expected values is possible because X_{ki} is itself a continuous measure, presenting an unlimited number of potential values.

When we deal with dummy variables, the independent variables are discrete measures limited to two possible values. In modeling a continuous dependent variable as a function of a single dummy variable (D_{ji}), we cannot claim to produce a regression line. Instead, we produce an expected (or predicted) value of Y_i for each of these two possible values: the predicted value of Y_i when $D_{ji} = 1$ and the predicted value of Y_i when $D_{ji} = 0$. These predicted values correspond to conditional means: the mean of Y_i for subgroup j.

To see how this works, consider the following three models involving INCOME (Y_i), a dummy variable for race (BLACK), and dummy variables for occupation (OCC$_2$ through OCC$_6$):

Model 1: $Y_i = f(\text{race}) = \beta_0 + \beta_1 \text{BLACK} + u_i$

Model 2: $Y_i = f(\text{occupation}) = \beta_0 + \beta_1 \text{OCC}_2 + \beta_2 \text{OCC}_3 + \beta_3 \text{OCC}_4 + \beta_4 \text{OCC}_5 + \beta_5 \text{OCC}_6 + u_i$

Model 3: $Y_i = f(\text{race, occupation}) = \beta_0 + \beta_1 \text{BLACK} + \beta_2 \text{OCC}_2 + \beta_3 \text{OCC}_3 + \beta_4 \text{OCC}_4 + \beta_5 \text{OCC}_5 + \beta_6 \text{OCC}_6 + u_i .$

Regression With One Dummy Variable

In Model 1, INCOME is regressed on BLACK to determine whether race is a useful predictor of earnings income. Results from this regression are presented in the first column of Table 3.1. An interpretation of

TABLE 3.1

Regression Results for Models 1, 2, and 3

	Model 1	Model 2	Model 3
Constant	7,821.9	10,702.1	10,811.4
	(91.9)	(160.8)	(158.9)
BLACK	−3,202.9		−1,676.0
	(171.6)		(172.4)
OCC_2		−3,021.2	−2,842.1
		(274.4)	(271.1)
OCC_3		−3,757.1	−3,566.4
		(215.5)	(213.3)
OCC_4		−5,148.2	−4,604.5
		(216.8)	(220.9)
OCC_5		−6,267.7	−5,512.7
		(289.7)	(295.9)
OCC_6		−6,612.1	−5,647.8
		(272.3)	(286.2)
R^2	.09792	.22400	.24624
F	348.3	185.0	174.4
Change from R_1^2			.148
F (change)			126.1

Variance/Covariance Matrix of Regression Coefficients for Model 2

	OCC_2	OCC_3	OCC_4	OCC_5	OCC_6
OCC_2	75,309.07				
OCC_3	25,870.70	46,439.50			
OCC_4	25,870.70	25,870.70	47,013.76		
OCC_5	25,870.70	25,870.70	25,870.70	83,922.03	
OCC_6	25,870.70	25,870.70	25,870.70	25,870.70	74,162.67

NOTE: Estimated regression coefficients, with standard errors (in parentheses).

these coefficients that is appropriate for both continuous and discrete independent variables is to regard the constant (B_0) as the expected value of Y_i when all independent variables are equal to zero, and B_1 as the change in the expected value of Y_i for each unit change in X_k. When X_k is continuous, the distribution of predicted Y_i values is also continuous; therefore, the regression coefficient indicates a slope. In contrast, when X_k is a dummy variable, the predicted value of Y_i changes by B_k units each time membership in the specified category is switched on or off, because a "unit" change in a dummy variable (from 0 to 1 or from 1 to 0) indicates membership or nonmembership in the designated category.

In this example, the negative coefficient for BLACK indicates that predicted income for respondents who are black is $3,202.90 less than predicted income for whites. Calculating predicted values of Y_i relies on routine substitution. When BLACK = 1, predicted income equals B_0 + B_1, or 7,821.9 − 3,202.9 = $4,619. When BLACK = 0, predicted income equals B_0 or $7,821.90. The reader can verify that these predicted values are the same values as the subgroup means reported in Table 2.2.

Significance tests for dummy variable coefficients follow standard procedures. The coefficient for BLACK measures the effect of being black rather than white on expected INCOME; therefore, the standard error of the coefficient for BLACK provides the standard error of the difference between expected income for whites and expected income for blacks. When testing against a null hypothesis of a zero effect (i.e., no subgroup difference in expected INCOME), the t test reduces to the ratio of the coefficient to the standard error. Similarly, because Model 1 contains a single independent variable, the F test for the model is a test of the same null hypothesis, and the value of F is the square of the t value. The information of R^2—that racial differences explain almost 10% of the variation in INCOME—was already established through the earlier examination of zero-order correlation coefficients.

This initial example has illustrated both the similarities and differences of regression interpretation when the independent variable is a dummy variable rather than a quantitative measure. The constant estimates the expected value of Y_i for the reference group (whites); B_1 estimates the effect of displaying the trait indicated by the dummy variable (i.e., the effect of being black). This effect captures the difference in expected INCOME for blacks and whites. Therefore, the null hypothesis that $\beta_1 = 0$ in Model 1 is equivalent to the null hypothesis, $H_0: \mu_{\text{BLACKS}} - \mu_{\text{WHITES}} = 0$. Both the t test for B_1 and the F test for Model 1 are essentially difference of means tests.[4]

Regression With Multiple Dummy Variables

Model 2 estimates INCOME as a function of occupational category represented by the five dummy variables already described. Results from this regression are reported in the middle column of Table 3.1. Consistent with the interpretation provided for Model 1, the value of the constant, 10,702.1, reports expected income for upper white-collar workers (the reference group). Remaining regression coefficients estimate the effect of being in a particular occupational category compared with the reference category. The coefficient for OCC_2 tells us that, on average, lower white-collar workers earn \$3,021.20 less than upper white-collar workers, or \$7,680.90. In contrast, laborers average \$6,612.10 less than upper white-collar workers, or only \$4,090.

Because distinctions among occupational groups are captured by the entire set of dummy variables rather than by any single dummy variable, the appropriate significance test for the effect of occupational category on INCOME is the F test for the model. As a test of the null hypothesis that β_1 through β_5 in Model 2 are simultaneously zero, the F test is a test of the hypothesis that the expected value of INCOME for all occupational groups is the same. In addition, as the F test can be expressed as the ratio of R^2 (divided by k degrees of freedom, where k equals the number of independent variables) to $1 - R^2$ (divided by $N - k - 1$ degrees of freedom), the F test can also be considered a test of the significance of R^2. Therefore, rejection of the null hypothesis suggests that a nonzero amount of variation in INCOME is explained by the respondent's occupational location. Based on results for Model 2, we have

$$F_{5,3205} = \frac{.22400/5}{(1 - .22400)/3205} = 185.0,$$

which is significant at better than the .001 level.[5] Having established the statistical significance of occupation, we can now turn to the t tests for individual coefficients that show that the expected INCOME for each included occupational category is significantly different from that of the reference group.

Assessing Differences
Between Specified Categories

The t tests associated with the regression coefficients of dummy variables allow us to test the significance of the effect of being in the designated category rather than in the reference group. However, it is not immediately apparent whether the included categories are different from each other. For example, OCC_6 (laborers) has the largest negative regression coefficient and therefore the lowest expected income. But how do we know if the expected income for laborers is smaller than the expected income for service workers, or for operatives?

Because $\beta_j = E(Y_i|OCC_j = 1) - E(Y_i|ref)$, the difference in expected income for included categories is equal to the difference between their coefficients, $(\beta_j - \beta_k)$, where β_j refers to the regression coefficient for a dummy variable designating category j and β_k is the regression coefficient for a dummy variable designating a different category. In order to test for a difference in the effects of OCC_4 and OCC_6 (the effect of being an operative rather than a laborer), we must use a t test for the difference in regression coefficients:

$$t = (B_j - B_k)/[\text{var}(B_j) + \text{var}(B_k) - 2\text{cov}(B_j B_k)]^{1/2}. \qquad [3.1]$$

As the variances of the coefficients are simply their squared standard errors, they are routinely available. In addition, many statistical packages provide the option of printing the variance/covariance matrix of regression coefficients, allowing the researcher the flexibility to compute these additional tests.[6]
Substituting estimated values for OCC_4 and OCC_6 into Equation 3.1, for example, we have:

$$t = -6,612.1 - (-5,148.2)/[74,162.7 + 47,013.8 - 2(25,870.7)]^{1/2}$$
$$= -1,463.9/263.5 = -5.56. \qquad [3.2]$$

Using the conventional $\alpha = .05$ to determine critical t values of ± 1.96, it is clear that the effect of being a laborer differs from the effect of being an operative—that is, that laborers and operatives do average different levels of income.

Adding a Second Qualitative Measure

Recall that when we looked at the subgroup means in Table 2.2, it was clear that as we moved from upper white-collar workers to laborers, not only did the average earnings decline, but the proportion of workers who were black increased. We may want to determine whether the racial differences in INCOME persist when we control for income differences in occupation. To answer this question, we must examine the partial regression coefficient for BLACK, controlling for occupation. Model 3 describes the appropriate specification, and the right-hand column of Table 3.1 reports the results. The constant, 10,811.4, indicates expected income when all independent variables are set to zero—in other words, expected income for upper white-collar workers who are white. The coefficient for BLACK, $-1,676.0$, indicates that once we take into account the variation in INCOME that is linked to occupational category and the fact that blacks are not uniformly distributed across all occupational categories, blacks still average $1,676 less income than whites. (Though smaller than was estimated in Model 1, this estimated difference in INCOME remains significant at better than the .001 level. The reduction in the magnitude of the coefficient for BLACK suggests that one reason blacks average lower incomes than whites is because they are concentrated in occupations in which workers, in general, have lower earnings.) Similarly, the partial regression coefficients associated with occupation dummy variables estimate the effect of membership in each of the designated categories (rather than in the reference group) on expected INCOME, controlling for racial differences in both INCOME and the distribution of respondents across occupational categories.

In deciding whether the partial effects of race (controlling for occupation) or the partial effects of occupation (controlling for race) are statistically significant, it is again appropriate to examine an F test. Rather than rely on the F test for the equation as a whole, however, we use the incremental F test to examine the explanatory power of one or a set of categorical variables, while controlling for other variables. For example, we can view Model 3 as a combination of the previous two models in which we add dummy variables denoting occupational category to a specification of racial differences. As before, the explanatory power of occupational location is captured by the set of dummy variables rather than by any single dummy variable. Therefore, we can assess the contribution of occupational location to the model by comparing the values of R^2 (or the mean regression sums of squares) between Model 3 and Model 1. The null hypothesis states that β_2 through β_6 (as specified in Model 3) are simultaneously zero—in other words, that once we control for racial differences in both INCOME and occupational location, the expected value of earned income is the same across occupational categories. The form of the test is

$$F = \frac{(R_3^2 - R_1^2)/(k_3 - k_1)}{(1 - R_3^2)/(N - k_3 - 1)} , \qquad [3.3]$$

where R_3^2 is the value of R^2 in Model 3, R_1^2 is the comparable measure in Model 1, N is the number of cases, and k_1 and k_3 are the number of independent variables included in Models 1 and 3, respectively. The numerator calculates the increment to R^2 that results from specifying the effects of occupational location relative to the difference in the number of independent variables between Model 3 and Model 1. The denominator is the proportion of variance left unexplained when both race and occupation are included (from Model 3) divided by the appropriate degrees of freedom. In our example, the increment to R^2 that results from adding OCC_2 through OCC_6 to the specification is .14832, divided by five degrees of freedom; therefore the F test for the significance of occupation controlling for race is

$$F = (.14832/5)/(.75376/3,204) = 126.1.$$

Predicted Values

Because race, with 2 categories, and occupation, with 6 categories, generate 12 distinct subgroups, Model 3 estimates 12 different values for predicted INCOME. These predicted values correspond to 12 subgroup means: 1 mean for each of the race-by-occupation subgroups. Using the combination of coefficients described in Table 3.2, the reader can reproduce the predicted values of INCOME for the various subgroups and compare the calculated values to the subgroup means reported in Table 2.2. Recall that the predicted values generated from Model 1 and Model 2 reproduced the subgroup means by race (when based on estimates from Model 1) or by occupation (when based on estimates from Model 2), as reported in Table 2.2. Unlike those earlier results, however, it is immediately apparent that the 12 predicted values of INCOME generated from Model 3 do not match the race-by-occupation subgroup means reported in Table 2.2. Why the difference?

In Models 1 and 2, we limited our examination to one dimension—*either* race *or* occupation. When we expanded the specification in Model 3, we did so under a simplifying assumption—namely, that the effect of BLACK (i.e., the estimated income difference between blacks and whites) is the same across all occupational groups, and that income differences across occupational groups are the same for whites and blacks. We can see this assumption at work when we calculate the predicted incomes for blacks and whites in various occupational groups: The difference between white workers and black workers is always 1,676 (the value of B_1), regardless of occupation; the difference between

TABLE 3.2
Predicted Values of Income From Model 3

	Blacks	Whites
OCC_1	$B_0 + B_1 = 9{,}135.4$	$B_0 = 10{,}811.4$
OCC_2	$B_0 + B_1 + B_2 = 6{,}293.3$	$B_0 + B_2 = 7{,}969.3$
OCC_3	$B_0 + B_1 + B_3 = 5{,}569.0$	$B_0 + B_3 = 7{,}245.0$
OCC_4	$B_0 + B_1 + B_4 = 4{,}530.9$	$B_0 + B_4 = 6{,}206.9$
OCC_5	$B_0 + B_1 + B_5 = 3{,}622.7$	$B_0 + B_5 = 5{,}298.7$
OCC_6	$B_0 + B_1 + B_6 = 3{,}487.6$	$B_0 + B_6 = 5{,}163.6$

service workers and upper white-collar workers is $-5{,}512.7$ (the value of B_5), regardless of race. This equivalence of effect is a function of model specification.

Is the simplifying assumption built into the specification of Model 3 empirically defensible? The fact that predicted incomes for subgroups differ from the subgroup means in Table 2.2 suggests that we may want to change the specification. A later model (Model 5) will provide a formal test of whether Model 3 or a model that allows differential effects (i.e., interactions) is preferable.

Adding Quantitative Variables to the Specification

A benefit of using regression analysis even when some independent variables are categorical is the flexibility of the modeling procedure. Up to this point, we have limited our initial models to dummy variable regressors, in order to allow the reader to become accustomed to the interpretation of dummy variable coefficients. It is now time to expand the specification and include both quantitative and dummy variable regressors. Model 4 defines INCOME as a function of race, occupation, education, and job tenure.

Model 4: $Y_i = f(\text{race, occupation, education, tenure})$
$$= \beta_0 + \beta_1 \text{BLACK} + \beta_2 \text{OCC}_2 + \beta_3 \text{OCC}_3 + \beta_4 \text{OCC}_4$$
$$+ \beta_5 \text{OCC}_5 + \beta_6 \text{OCC}_6 + \beta_7 \text{EDUC} + \beta_8 \text{TENURE} + u_i$$

Both EDUC and TENURE are treated as quantitative independent variables measured in years. Results for Model 4 are reported in Table 3.3.

TABLE 3.3
Regression Results for Model 4

Constant	5,761.1
	(359.0)
BLACK	−1,188.1
	(169.4)
OCC_2	−2,316.1
	(261.8)
OCC_3	−2,343.7
	(223.7)
OCC_4	−3,166.6
	(237.5)
OCC_5	−3,918.5
	(299.9)
OCC_6	−3,606.8
	(306.4)
EDUC	282.0
	(23.1)
TENURE	84.7
	(6.6)
R^2	.31459
F	183.7
R^2 change from Model 3	.068
F (change)	159.7***

NOTE: Regression coefficients with standard errors (in parentheses).
***Coefficient is statistically significant at the .001 level.

The value of the constant is considerably smaller than in previous estimations; more important, the change in specification has also changed its substantive meaning. The constant now estimates expected income for white upper white-collar workers who have zero years of schooling and zero years of tenure on the job—an unlikely combination of traits. The coefficient for BLACK now estimates the difference between expected income for blacks and whites once variation in income caused by occupation, education, and job tenure has been partialed out (i.e., $1,188.10). Coefficients for occupational dummy variables estimate the net difference in expected income for each occupational group relative to the reference group, controlling for other independent variables in the equation; for example, lower white-collar workers average $2,316.10 less in expected income than upper white-collar workers, and so on. Similarly, with race, occupation, and education held constant, each additional year on the job translates into another $84.70 in earnings.

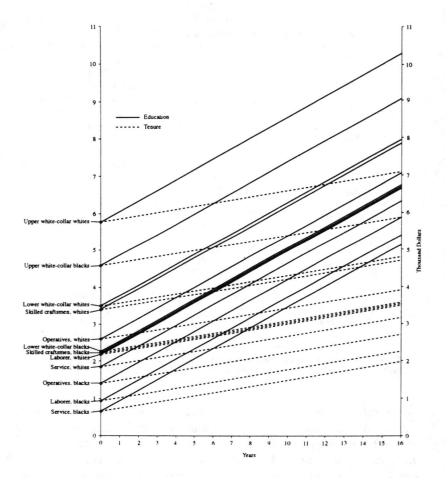

Figure 3.1. Results of Model 4

Under comparable conditions, an additional year of education is associated with an increase of $282 in expected income.

Given the addition of two quantitative independent variables to the specification, we can think of Model 4 as generating a series of regression planes and reintroduce the notions of intercept and slope or partial slope. Within this context, we can think of the coefficients of the dummy variables as denoting differential intercepts. Slopes, or partial slopes, can be associated only with quantitative independent variables; therefore, the coefficients associated with EDUC and TENURE provide estimates of partial slopes. Figure 3.1 illustrates the results of Model 4. In order to allow the reader to compare the intercept values and partial slopes for education and job tenure quickly across subgroups, Figure 3.1 represents these relationships as lines in two-dimensional space rather than planes in three-dimensional space. Because both education and job tenure are measured in years, we can represent their partial effects relative to the same scale.

Because the specification constrains estimation to an average effect of education and an average effect of tenure across all respondents, all solid lines have the same slope ($282 per year) and all broken lines have the same slope ($84.70 per year). However, the Y intercepts are allowed to differ by subgroup. Twelve separate intercepts are specified. Calculation of these intercept values uses the same combination of coefficients described in Table 3.2; however, because the values of the coefficients themselves have changed as a result of the expanded specification, the calculated intercepts will differ from the predicted dollar values reported in Table 3.2. From each of the intercepts characterizing a particular race-by-occupation subgroup emanates one solid line and one broken line representing the partial effects of education and job tenure, respectively. For each race-by-occupation subgroup, we can identify (a) the appropriate Y intercept (the expected value of Y for a member of a given subgroup with zero years of education and zero years of job tenure), (b) the net change in the expected value of Y predicted for an additional year of education for a particular subgroup (the solid line), and (c) the net change in the expected value of Y predicted for an additional year of job tenure for a particular subgroup (the broken line). As was the case in Model 3, the equivalence of effect across subgroups is an assumption embedded in the model specification; its empirical adequacy remains to be tested.

4. ASSESSING GROUP
DIFFERENCES IN EFFECTS

The models in the previous chapter were developed by expanding the number and types of independent variables included in the specification. All multivariate models shared the simplifying assumption that the effect of any single explanatory variable was the same across the range of any other explanatory variable. In other words, we included no interaction terms to test whether the effect of occupation, education, or tenure differed for blacks and whites. In this chapter, we develop models to test the validity of that assumption by introducing interaction terms into the specification. We then return to two issues that were introduced earlier in the text—the consequences of violating assumptions of the regression model and alternative approaches to making multiple comparisons with nonindependent tests.

Estimating average effects across subgroups can often give a useful and parsimonious description of relationships. Occasionally, however, an independent variable (X_i) has a differential effect on Y_i across categories or values of a second independent variable (Z_i). When the relationship between X_i and Y_i depends on the value of Z_i, we must adjust model specification to allow the X_iY_i relationship to vary relative to values on Z_i. Testing for these differential effects involves the use of interaction terms—terms defined as the product of two or more independent variables already included in the specification.

Interaction terms may be defined as the product of two quantitative variables, of two dummy variables, or of one quantitative and one dummy variable. In addition, more complex interactions may involve more than two variables. In an earlier contribution to this series, Jaccard, Turrisi, and Wan (1990) provide an excellent discussion of interaction effects when all variables involved are continuous measures. We will be concerned with the other combinations.

Consider first an interaction that involves two dummy variables (D_{1i}, D_{2i}) that have been constructed to measure the effects of two dichotomous qualitative variables, gender and marital status. We might hypothesize, for example, that the effect of being female (rather than male) depends on whether you are married or unmarried. Under these circumstances, we would want to test a model that specifies the effect of being female (by including D_{1i}), the effect of being married (by including D_{2i}), and the interaction effect (by including the product variable $D_{1i} \times D_{2i}$, which equals 1 when a respondent is both female and married). The coefficient for the interaction term estimates the extent to which the effect of being female differs for married and nonmarried sample members.

Now consider an interaction term defined by one quantitative variable (X_i) measuring age and our dummy variable D_{1i} for gender. Here, we might hypothesize that the effect of age depends on whether one is a man or a women. We would therefore want to specify a model that estimates the effect of age (by including X_i), the effect of gender (by including D_{1i}), and the interaction effect (by including the product variable $X_i \times D_{1i}$). Here, the interaction is equal to zero for all men; for women, it assumes the value of their age. The coefficient for the interaction term estimates the extent to which the effect of age for women is smaller (or greater) than the effect of age for men.

Consideration of Figure 3.1 will help us conceptualize the types of differential effects we may wish to examine in our illustrative data on earnings among older male workers. We can see in Figure 3.1 that, because of the way we specified Models 3 and 4, the income gap between white and black workers belonging to the same occupational group was constant for all occupations. Is it possible that the income disadvantage associated with being black is larger among upper white-collar workers and smaller among laborers? In other words, is it possible that the gap between the Y intercepts for upper white-collar workers is wider than the gap between Y intercepts for the two groups of laborers? A more general expression of this question asks whether the effect of race may vary by occupational group or, equivalently, whether the income advantage of being employed in certain types of occupations operates the same for blacks and whites.

To gain a better understanding of some possible types of interaction effects involving qualitative variables, let us turn to Table 4.1, which displays three versions of the relationships among income, race, and occupation. Each of the three parts of the table reports race-by-occupation subgroup means on INCOME. Marginal values by row report mean income by race; marginal values by column report mean income by occupational category. The first two sections of the table contain hypothetical data constructed to illustrate types of interaction effects yet preserve the same subgroup means for each occupation. By reviewing these, we can see that the marginal differences in income between blacks and whites (reported to the far right) do not always accurately capture the relationships among race, occupation, and income described within each section.

For example, the set of data in the top of the table displays no interaction effects. When no interaction effects exist, the difference in mean income between blacks and whites reflected in the marginal values ($3,203) is exactly the same size as the difference found when one compares mean income for blacks and whites within columns (i.e., controlling for occupation category). The reader can verify this claim by subtracting means in the first row from means in the second row within each column. In this situation, the estimated effect of race in a

TABLE 4.1

Possible Types of Interaction Effects

	UWC	LWC	Skill	Oper	Serv	Labor	
No interaction effects[a]							
blacks	7,708	5,029	4,315	3,599	2,883	2,939	4,412
whites	10,911	8,232	7,518	6,802	6,086	6,142	7,615
	10,702	7,681	6,945	5,554	4,434	4,090	
Interaction effects involving a difference in magnitude and direction[a]							
blacks	7,002	5,851	5,158	6,111	5,120	4,628	5,470
whites	10,960	8,061	7,335	5,198	3,704	3,130	7,479
	10,702	7,681	6,945	5,554	4,434	4,090	
Interaction effects involving a difference in magnitude[b]							
blacks	7,002	5,851	5,158	4,721	4,086	3,704	4,619
whites	10,960	8,061	7,335	6,085	4,806	4,777	7,822
	10,702	7,681	6,945	5,554	4,434	4,090	

NOTE: a. Fabricated data.
b. Actual data.

regression model such as Model 3 (an effect that is averaged across all occupational groups) provides an accurate picture of black/white differences in earnings because the effect of race operates uniformly across all occupational categories.

The second part of Table 4.1, also based on fabricated data, illustrates a situation in which the effect of race differs in both magnitude and sign. With this type of interaction, not only the effect of race (the magnitude of the black/white difference in average income) varies across categories of occupation; the designation of advantage also varies. Suppose subgroup means for our sample of workers were arrayed as they are in the middle of Table 4.1. In this example, the marginal difference in income by race (or the average effect of race) is $2,009, with whites averaging higher incomes. But as we look within the table (i.e., as we condition our comparison on specific occupational groups), we find that the magnitude of the income gap between whites and blacks is not always the same. The gap is widest among upper white-collar workers ($3,958) and smallest among operatives ($913). Because the income gap between whites and blacks does not appear to be uniform across occupational groups, we identify an interaction effect. Further, the income gap is not always in the same direction. Whites average higher earnings only in the upper white-collar, lower white-collar, and skilled categories. Among operatives, service workers, and laborers, blacks average higher incomes. It is the shift in the direction of the difference that characterizes this particular type of interaction effect. The marginal difference between incomes for whites and blacks therefore obscures some important aspects of the race effect. By averaging across all occupational groups, we are left with a summary race effect that is reasonably accurate (in this hypothetical case) for lower white-collar and skilled workers, but an underestimate of the race difference among upper white-collar workers and an estimate in the wrong direction for remaining categories of workers.

The bottom part of Table 4.1 allows us to compare values from our actual data with the fabricated alternative distributions. The values of mean income for this section are also found in Table 2.2. In our actual data, the marginal difference in income between blacks and whites is $3,203 (the difference we estimated in the first regression model). But when we look within occupational groups, we see that the difference in income between blacks and whites depends on the occupational category. The gap is largest among upper white-collar workers ($3,958) and smallest among service workers ($720). However, the income difference is always in the same direction—black workers always average smaller incomes. When dealing with this type of interaction, the average effect is always in the correct direction, but for some occupational categories the estimate is too small and for others it is too large.

Specifying Interaction Effects

In order to test for interaction effects, we require a specification that allows us to estimate differential effects and then ascertain their significance. We accomplish this goal by constructing five product terms and adding these terms to the specification. Model 5 allows us to test for the differential effects of race by occupation or, equivalently, the differential effects of occupation by race.

Model 5: $Y_i = f(\text{race, occ, educ, tenure})$
$$\begin{aligned}
= &\ \beta_0 + \beta_1\text{BLACK} + \beta_2\text{OCC}_2 + \beta_3\text{OCC}_3 + \beta_4\text{OCC}_4 \\
&+ \beta_5\text{OCC}_5 + \beta_6\text{OCC}_6 + \beta_7\text{EDUC} + \beta_8\text{TENURE} \\
&+ \beta_9\text{BLOCC}_2 + \beta_{10}\text{BLOCC}_3 + \beta_{11}\text{BLOCC}_4 \\
&+ \beta_{12}\text{BLOCC}_5 + \beta_{13}\text{BLOCC}_6 + u_i
\end{aligned}$$

The new variables, BLOCC_2 through BLOCC_6, are computed by multiplying BLACK with each of the occupational dummy variables.

TABLE 4.2
Regression Results for Model 5

Constant	5,794.8
	(358.7)
BLACK	-3,793.3
	(610.1)
OCC_2	-2,274.9
	(280.2)
OCC_3	-2,418.4
	(232.7)
OCC_4	-3,427.2
	(256.3)
OCC_5	-4,513.4
	(372.5)
OCC_6	-4,202.8
	(399.0)
EDUC	292.9
	(23.1)
TENURE	84.0
	(6.6)
$BLOCC_2$	1,501.2
	(823.0)
$BLOCC_3$	2,326.2
	(705.0)
$BLOCC_4$	2,984.8
	(672.5)
$BLOCC_5$	3,528.0
	(761.0)
$BLOCC_6$	3,383.9
	(747.3)
R^2	.32138
F	116.46
R^2 change from Model 4	.007
F (change)	6.42***

NOTE: Regression coefficients with standard errors (in parentheses).
***Coefficient is statistically significant at the .001 level.

For example, the product variable $BLOCC_2$ is coded 1 if the respondent is both black *and* in a lower white-collar job; therefore the increment or decrement to average earnings estimated by the coefficient for $BLOCC_2$ applies only to this distinct subset—black workers in lower white-collar positions.

Results from Model 5 are presented in Table 4.2. Initially, we may want to know whether allowing differential effects of race and occupation resulted in a statistically significant improvement in the fit of the model. We can answer this question by performing the increment to R^2 test described in Equation 3.3. Comparing results from Model 5 to those reported for Model 4, we have

$$F_{5, 3197} = \frac{.00679/5}{.67862/3,197} = 6.4,$$

an F value that is statistically significant at better than the .001 level. Although the increment to explanatory power is far from overwhelming, the F test does suggest that the large sample size has enabled us to estimate differential effects with reasonable accuracy.

Turning to the set of regression coefficients, the interpretation of the constant is the same as it was in Model 4—predicted income for white upper white-collar workers with zero years of education and tenure. In addition, the coefficient for EDUC reports the average effect of education on income, controlling for job tenure, race, occupation, and the differential effects of race within occupational groups. The interpretation of the coefficient for TENURE is comparable.

Although coefficients for BLACK and the occupation dummy variables may appear to carry over from Model 4, they do not. Because of the inclusion of the race-by-occupation product terms, their meaning has changed. As we continue to work with 12 race-by-occupation subgroups, we can explicate the role played by each particular coefficient by mapping the coefficients to their respective subgroups. This mapping, reported in Table 4.3, is constructed by including a given coefficient in the estimate of predicted INCOME for certain subgroups only if an individual from that subgroup is coded 1 on the given dummy variable (product variables included). For simplicity's sake we ignore, for the moment, coefficients for EDUC and TENURE, as if the values for these independent variables had been set to zero.

Beginning with the coefficient for BLACK, we see that B_1 estimates the difference in expected INCOME between black and white upper white-collar workers. It no longer provides an estimate of the average effect of BLACK across all occupational subgroups as it did in Model 4. The t test for this coefficient, then, is a test of the null hypothesis that, after having controlled for variation in income due to education and tenure, expected income for black upper white-collar workers is equal to the expected income for white upper white-collar workers—in other words, that BLACK has no significant effect on expected income

TABLE 4.3

Coefficients Used to Predict INCOME for
Race-by-Occupation Subgroups

	Whites	Blacks
Upper white-collar	B_0	$B_0 + B_1$
Lower white-collar	$B_0 + B_2$	$B_0 + B_1 + B_2 + B_9$
Skilled	$B_0 + B_3$	$B_0 + B_1 + B_3 + B_{10}$
Operative	$B_0 + B_4$	$B_0 + B_1 + B_4 + B_{11}$
Service	$B_0 + B_5$	$B_0 + B_1 + B_5 + B_{12}$
Laborer	$B_0 + B_6$	$B_0 + B_1 + B_6 + B_{13}$

(net of other variables) for upper white-collar workers. Because this null hypothesis can be rejected (the t value for this coefficient is −6.22), we learn that, among upper white-collar workers, blacks average significantly lower incomes, controlling for all other factors specified in the model.

In a similar way, the coefficients for the occupation dummy variables no longer provide an estimate of the average effect (for whites and blacks together) of being in a particular occupational category (versus the reference group). Instead, B_2 (the coefficient for OCC_2) estimates the difference in expected earnings between lower white-collar and upper white-collar workers who are white: White lower white-collar workers average $2,274.90 less in INCOME than white upper white-collar workers. Likewise, white operatives average $3,427.20 less in INCOME than white upper white-collar workers. In other words, once product terms are specified, the coefficients for the original set of variables (in this case, BLACK and OCC_2 through OCC_6) refer to comparisons involving the reference categories: B_1 measures the effect of being BLACK for upper white-collar workers (the reference category for occupation); B_2 through B_6 measure the effects of occupying an occupational category other than upper white-collar for white workers (the reference category for race). The t tests associated with the regression coefficients for OCC_2 through OCC_6 are therefore tests for significant differences among occupational groups for white workers that can be generalized to the population. Results from Table 4.2 indicate that the estimated differences between upper white-collar workers and other categories of occupation are significantly different from zero for white workers.

The regression coefficients for the product variables estimate the differential effect of occupation by race. Alternatively, we can view these coefficients as estimates of the differential effect of being BLACK by occupational category. Why are both explanations acceptable? By reviewing Table 4.3 we can formulate an answer to that question. Whereas the difference in predicted INCOME between lower white-collar workers and upper white-collar workers among white respondents is captured by B_2 (−2,274.9), for blacks this contrast is captured by $B_2 + B_9$ (−2,274.9 + 1,501.2). Therefore B_9 estimates the difference in the effect of being lower white-collar workers (rather than upper white-collar workers) for blacks relative to whites. Because the coefficient for BLOCC$_2$ is positive, the earnings gap between lower white-collar workers and upper white-collar workers is $1,501.20 narrower for blacks than for whites, or −$773.70 rather than −$2,274.90. Similarly, the difference in expected INCOME between blacks and whites who are upper white-collar workers is B_1 (−3,793.3); but the black/white difference among lower white-collar workers is $B_1 + B_9$ (−3,793.3 + 1,501.2). B_9 estimates the difference in the effect of being black for lower white-collar workers relative to upper white-collar workers, a difference estimated as −3,793.3 for upper white-collar workers, but at −2,292.1 for lower white-collar workers. Therefore, differences in expected INCOME by occupation for black workers are captured by the sum of two coefficients $\beta_j + \beta_{jk}$, where β_j is the coefficient of an occupation dummy variable (OCC$_2$ through OCC$_6$) and β_{jk} is the coefficient of a product variable. We can define the connection between β_j and β_{jk} as follows:

$$\beta_j = E(Y_i|_{\text{WHITE,OCC}_j}) - E(Y_i|_{\text{WHITE,OCCref}}) \qquad [4.1]$$

$$\beta_{jk} = [E(Y_i|_{\text{BLACK,OCC}_j}) - E(Y_i|_{\text{BLACK,OCCref}})] \qquad [4.2]$$
$$- [E(Y_i|_{\text{WHITE,OCC}_j} - E(Y_i|_{\text{WHITE,OCCref}})]$$

$$= [E(Y_i|_{\text{BLACK,OCC}_j}) - E(Y_i|_{\text{BLACK,OCCref}})] - \beta_j. \qquad [4.3]$$

Therefore,

$$\beta_j + \beta_{jk} = E(Y_i|_{\text{BLACK,OCC}_j}) - E(Y_i|_{\text{BLACK,OCCref}}). \qquad [4.4]$$

As we can see from Equation 4.2, the t tests reported for the regression coefficients of product terms are not tests of the significance of net occupational differences in expected INCOME among blacks. Instead, the hypotheses being tested investigate whether the net income differential between specific occupational groups and the reference group is the same for blacks and whites.

If the coefficients for these product terms had been negative, we would have had evidence that the earnings differences between upper white-collar workers and remaining occupational groups were larger for blacks than for whites; that is, the occupational differences in earnings that had been identified for whites (through the negative coefficients for OCC_2 through OCC_6) would have been even larger for blacks (through the extra negative effect captured by coefficients for the product terms). Because these coefficients are positive, it appears that the differences in earnings across occupational groups are more pronounced for white workers, more compact for black workers; in fact, there may be no significant occupational differences in INCOME among black workers. It also seems that the black/white difference in expected INCOME becomes narrower as we move down the occupational scale.

Let's examine each of these tentative conclusions more carefully. To address the former of these two conclusions, we must determine whether there are significant occupational differences (once education and job tenure are controlled) in expected INCOME among African Americans. None of the t tests routinely provided for coefficient estimates by computer programs allows us to answer this question. The t tests for the interaction terms tell us whether the net effects of occupation are significantly different for blacks and whites. However, knowing that the net effect of being either a skilled worker, an operative, a service worker, or a laborer rather than an upper white-collar worker differs by race does not in itself allow us to determine whether the net effect of being in one occupational category rather than another is a reliable predictor of INCOME among blacks. To answer this question, we must go one step further.

In Table 4.4 we examine the race-specific effects of occupation for blacks and whites, controlling for education and job tenure. The entries for whites are the same as the coefficients for OCC_2, OCC_3, OCC_4, OCC_5, and OCC_6 in Table 4.2 because these coefficients estimate the contrast between the reference group and other occupational groups for whites. Recall that reported tests of statistical significance for these coefficients indicate whether net occupational differences exist for white workers in the population. In addition, if we wanted to test whether white operatives average lower incomes than white skilled workers—that is, to look at occupational differences in expected IN-COME between these two occupational groups while controlling for

TABLE 4.4

Net Effects of Occupation on INCOME by Race

	Whites	Blacks[a]
Lower white-collar	-2,274.9	-773.7
	(280.2)	(776.7)
Skilled	-2,418.4	-92.2
	(232.7)	(683.5)
Operative	-3,427.2	-442.4
	(256.3)	(646.5)
Service	-4,513.4	-985.4
	(372.5)	(682.6)
Laborer	-4,202.8	-818.9
	(399.0)	(667.6)

NOTE: a. Entries for blacks were calculated by summing coefficients; standard errors were calculated as $[\mathrm{var}(B_i) + \mathrm{var}(B_j) + 2\,\mathrm{cov}(B_i, B_j)]^{1/2}$.

race, education, and job tenure—we would use Equation 3.1, the coefficients $B_3 = -2,418.4$ and $B_4 = -3,427.2$ from Model 5, and their respective variances and covariance.

For blacks, the effects of being in one occupational category rather than another are captured by two sets of coefficients: the coefficients for the occupational dummy variables and the coefficients for the race-by-occupation interaction terms. For example, to determine how black lower white-collar workers and black upper white-collar workers differ in terms of predicted INCOME, we must sum B_2 (the difference between expected INCOME for upper and lower white-collar workers among whites) and B_9 (the measure of how the INCOME contrast between upper and lower white-collar workers differs for blacks relative to whites). Referring to Table 4.3, we see that, among blacks, calculating the expected INCOME for lower white-collar workers uses the same two coefficients as the upper white-collar category plus two more—$B_2 + B_9$.[7] Therefore, for blacks, the estimated effects of being in one of the occupational categories included in Table 4.4 rather than the upper white-collar reference category are constructed by summing appropriate pairs of coefficients.

As we can see from Table 4.4, the earnings disadvantage associated with not being an upper white-collar worker appears much smaller for blacks than for whites. In contrast to the occupational differences reported for whites, the smallest difference for blacks is between upper white-collar and skilled blue-collar workers rather than between categories of white-collar workers. In fact, among blacks, the net difference in income between upper and lower white-collar workers is approximately the same as the difference between upper white-collar workers and laborers. However, these estimates of the net occupational differences in predicted income for blacks are based only on the regression coefficients. Do inference tests give us confidence in these estimated differences, or can they be largely attributed to sampling error?

The t tests for the coefficients of the product terms in Table 4.2 told us that the income gaps between specified occupational groups and upper white-collar workers were significantly different for blacks and whites in all but the lower white-collar/upper white-collar contrast. But we have as yet made no direct test of whether there are significant occupational differences in earnings among blacks. The required t test is one that assesses the sum of two coefficients relative to the standard deviation of the sampling distribution of this statistic, for example, $(B_2 + B_9)/\mathrm{SE}(B_2 + B_9)$. The following formula, similar to the one presented in Equation 3.1, serves the purpose:

$$t = B_j + B_{jk} / [\mathrm{var}(B_j) + \mathrm{var}(B_{jk}) + 2\mathrm{cov}(B_j, B_{jk})]^{1/2} . \qquad [4.5]$$

Here, as in Equations 4.1 through 4.4, B_j refers to a coefficient for an occupation dummy variable referencing category j, and B_{jk} refers to the coefficient for a product variable between the kth independent variable (in this example, BLACK) and the occupation dummy variable referencing category j. The t tests reported in the column for blacks in Table 4.4 were calculated by substituting into Equation 4.5. None of the reported t values exceeds the critical values of ±1.96. The conclusion we would draw from these results is that, although occupational location has a significant effect (net of education and job tenure) on the expected earnings level for workers who are white, occupation does not reliably improve prediction of average income among blacks.[8]

At this point, let us return to Figure 3.1. We began this chapter by hypothesizing that the effect of occupation varies by race. In terms of the figure, we proposed that the race differences in intercepts would not be the same across all occupational categories. The model we estimated to examine this hypothesis allowed us to conclude that, in fact, we were correct: Income differences between occupational groups were not of the same magnitude for black and white workers. A comparison of Figure 4.1 with Figure 3.1 should make that point clear.

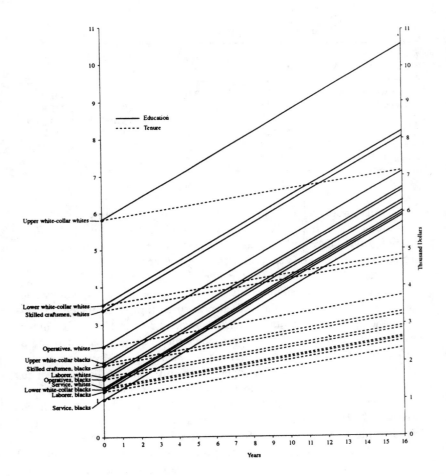

Figure 4.1. Results of Model 5

As additional illustration, Table 4.5 contains estimated intercept values for each of the 12 subgroups depicted in Figures 3.1 and 4.1. The two columns on the left provide the intercepts calculated using estimates from Model 4 (those illustrated in Figure 3.1) and the two columns on the right provide the intercepts calculated using estimates from Model 5 (those illustrated in Figure 4.1). Because of the differential effect of race across occupational groups, the intercepts from Model

TABLE 4.5

Differential Intercepts by Race and Occupation

	Model 4		Model 5	
	Whites	*Blacks*	*Whites*	*Blacks*
Upper white-collar	5,761.1	4,573.0	5,794.8	2,001.5
Lower white-collar	3,445.0	2,256.9	3,519.9	1,227.8
Skilled	3,417.4	2,229.3	3,376.4	1,909.3
Operative	2,594.5	1,406.4	2,367.6	1,559.1
Service	1,842.6	654.5	1,281.4	1,016.1
Laborer	2,154.3	966.2	1,592.0	1,182.6

5 not only modify the distance between subgroups, they reorder the subgroups along the Y axis. (Keep in mind that these values reflect predicted INCOME for workers in the various race-by-occupation subgroups who have zero years of schooling and zero years of tenure.)

For example, in Figure 3.1 the vertical distance between the upper white-collar and the skilled craftsmen lines is the same for whites and blacks. For both groups, the skilled craftsmen line is displaced $2,344 below the upper white-collar line. This value, $2,344, is the coefficient for OCC_3 reported in Table 3.3 and estimates the average effect of being a craftsman rather than a professional on yearly earnings. However, in Figure 4.1, this same comparison of upper white-collar and skilled craftsmen categories illustrates the race-specific effects of occupation. For whites, the vertical distance between the two lines is $2,418; for blacks the distance is only $92. These values are directly obtained from Table 4.4, which is based on the regression results for Model 5 reported in Table 4.2.

Although the spacing of the intercepts differs from Figure 3.1 to Figure 4.1, in both cases the partial slopes for education and job tenure are the same across all subgroups: All solid lines continue to be parallel, indicating the average effect of education across all respondents; all broken lines continue to be parallel, indicating the average effect of job tenure. The last model to be developed in this chapter calls this point into question: Should the partial effects of education and tenure be the same for all subgroups? We can hypothesize race-specific effects for education and job tenure and then test to see if the effects of education and job tenure are the same for blacks and whites. Even if we find that the dividend for additional years of education or job tenure is different for blacks and whites, some lines will continue to be parallel. Because six sets of lines are for blacks (one for each occupational group) and six sets of lines are for whites (one for each occupational group), finding differential effects of education by race would argue only that all solid lines for black workers would be parallel to each other, and all solid lines for white workers would be parallel to each other, though at a different slope than the solid lines for blacks.[9] A similar situation would exist for job tenure.

To test the hypotheses that $\beta_{EDUC(whites)} = \beta_{EDUC(blacks)}$ and $\beta_{TENURE(whites)} = \beta_{TENURE(blacks)}$, we construct a model that allows us to estimate the difference in effects for whites and blacks. By adding two additional terms to Model 5, we can accomplish this task. Because we are testing the variability of relationships, we again utilize product terms. In this case, the product terms are created by multiplying EDUC by BLACK to make BLEDUC and TENURE by BLACK to make BLTEN. For blacks in the sample, the distribution of BLEDUC will be the same as the distribution for EDUC; however, whites in the sample will all be coded 0 on BLEDUC. The same applies to the distributions of BLTEN and TENURE. The model to be estimated is as follows:

Model 6: $Y_i = f$(race, occ, educ, tenure)
$$= \beta_0 + \beta_1 BLACK + \beta_2 OCC_2 + \beta_3 OCC_3 + \beta_4 OCC_4$$
$$+ \beta_5 OCC_5 + \beta_6 OCC_6 + \beta_7 EDUC + \beta_8 TENURE$$
$$+ \beta_9 BLOCC_2 + \beta_{10} BLOCC_3 + \beta_{11} BLOCC_4$$
$$+ \beta_{12} BLOCC_5 + \beta_{13} BLOCC_6 + \beta_{14} BLEDUC$$
$$+ \beta_{15} BLTENURE + u_i$$

Regression results for this model appear in Table 4.6. With the exception of EDUC and TENURE, the interpretation of the coefficients for variables included in Model 5 remain essentially the same in Model 6, with one qualification: We now assess these effects controlling for the differential impact of education and job tenure by race in addition to the other independent variables.

Although the coefficient estimates and significance tests for many of these variables remain largely unchanged, we note some differences between the regression results for Models 5 and 6. In particular, the coefficient for the dummy variable BLACK has been reduced by more than half, and it is no longer significant at the .05 level or better. In addition, the coefficient for the interaction term $BLOCC_3$ is noticeably smaller and only marginally significant. How can we explain these changes in results?

To answer that question we must look at the two "new" variables we added to the model—the interaction terms for education and job tenure.

TABLE 4.6
Regression Results for Model 6

		Effects for Blacks[a]
Constant	4,962.5	
	(435.9)	
Black	−1,667.3	
	(901.3)	
OCC$_2$	−2,155.4	−1,068.8
	(281.7)	(779.5)
OCC$_3$	−2,167.9	−718.4
	(242.5)	(703.4)
OCC$_4$	−3,132.1	−1,144.5
	(268.8)	(672.7)
OCC$_5$	−4,281.2	−1,605.1
	(378.9)	(703.4)
OCC$_6$	−3,851.3	−1,611.5
	(411.0)	(703.7)
EDUC	359.1	186.3
	(29.4)	(37.3)
TENURE	80.3	94.6
	(7.6)	(13.1)
BLOCC$_2$	1,086.5	
	(829.0)	
BLOCC$_3$	1,449.5	
	(744.4)	
BLOCC$_4$	1,987.6	
	(724.7)	
BLOCC$_5$	2,676.1	
	(799.5)	
BLOCC$_6$	2,239.7	
	(815.2)	
BLEDUC	−172.7	
	(47.5)	
BLTEN	14.2	
	(15.2)	
R^2	.32434	
F	102.25	
R^2 change from Model 5	.00296	
F change	7.01***	

NOTES: Regression coefficients with standard errors (in parentheses).
a. Entries for blacks were calculated by summing coefficients; standard errors were calculated as $[\text{var}(B_i) + \text{var}(B_j) + 2\,\text{cov}(B_i\,B_j)]^{1/2}$.
***Coefficient is statistically significant at the .001 level.

The coefficient for BLTENURE is nonsignificant, suggesting that additional tenure with the same employer "pays" black and white workers about equally. Under this new specification, the interpretation of the coefficient for TENURE is modified in the same way that the interpretation of the coefficients for OCC_2 through OCC_6 was modified when we moved from Model 4 to Model 5 and first introduced product terms. Here, the coefficient for TENURE estimates the effect of additional years with the same employer for white workers at $80.30 per year. The coefficient for BLTENURE estimates the difference between the net effect of job tenure for blacks and whites to be $14.20, making each additional year worth $94.50 for black workers. However, the size of the standard error for BLTENURE indicates that evidence of this difference in effect is weak. Therefore, we are led to the conclusion that tenure operates in roughly the same way for whites and blacks.

The situation with education is different. The coefficient for EDUC tells us that, controlling for the effects of other variables in the model, each additional year of education is associated with $359.10 in additional income for whites. The coefficient for BLEDUC indicates that for blacks, each additional year of schooling pays $172.70 less than that, or $186.40. The significance test for BLEDUC labels this difference statistically significant: In the population, an additional year of education was associated with a smaller average increment to income for blacks than for whites, net of other variables in the equation. Because the net effect of education does differ for blacks and whites, the estimated effect for education in Model 5 (the average effect of education for blacks and whites) underestimates the return on additional years of schooling for whites and overestimates the effect for blacks.

We can ask of these effects the same questions that we asked when we were addressing occupation-by-race interaction terms. Specifically, we know now that the net effect of tenure for blacks is not significantly different from the net effect of tenure for whites, but that the net effect of education is different for blacks. We do not know whether education significantly affects the expected level of income for blacks. To answer this question, we must return to Equation 4.4 and test the sum of the coefficients estimating the effect of education for blacks. Substituting into Equation 4.4, we find

$$t = 359.1 + (-172.7)/[(862.691) + (2,253.569) + 2(-862.691)]^{1/2}$$
$$= 186.4/37.29 = 5.00.$$

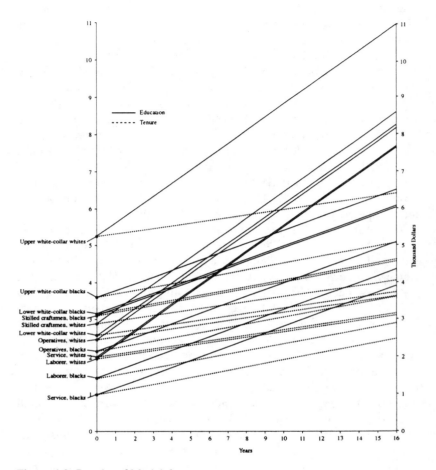

Figure 4.2. Results of Model 6

We can conclude that education does affect expected income for both whites and blacks; however, black workers average a lower rate of return on education than do white workers.

In response to our earlier question—How can we account for the shift in the effects of BLACK and BLOCC$_3$?—we can offer the following explanation. When we constrained the net effect of education on IN-COME to be the same for whites and blacks (as we did in Model 5), the coefficient for BLACK indicated that, among upper white-collar workers, blacks were at a significant earnings disadvantage; on average, upper white-collar workers who were black earned almost $4,000 less per year than upper white-collar workers who were white, controlling for other variables in the equation. Similarly, the net difference in expected INCOME for skilled workers and upper white-collar workers was much larger for whites ($2,418.40) than for blacks ($92.20). Both of these findings are reflected in Figure 4.1. However, once we estimate race-specific effects for education (as we do in Model 6), we find that, among upper white-collar workers, the net difference in expected IN-COME between blacks and whites is nonsignificant at the standard .05 level for a two-tailed test. Although the standard error for the coefficient for BLACK has increased from Model 5 to Model 6, the more important change is in the point estimate for the coefficient itself; the coefficient in Model 6 is less than half the size of the coefficient in Model 5. This reduction in size is reflected in the smaller gap between the Y intercepts for black versus white upper white-collar workers in Figure 4.2. But as we move across the horizontal axis to higher levels of education, the gap between solid lines for black versus white upper white-collar workers widens, suggesting that the relative earnings advantage of white upper white-collar workers over black upper white-collar workers increases with the level of education. For example, what was a difference of $1,667 (at zero years of education and job tenure, an unlikely set of values for upper white-collar workers) becomes an average difference of $4,430 for upper white-collar workers with 16 years of education.

Turning our attention to $BLOCC_3$, we find that the coefficient for $BLOCC_3$ in Model 6 is smaller than the coefficient reported for $BLOCC_3$ in Model 5; as a result, we can no longer reject the null hypothesis that the net effect of being a skilled worker rather than an upper white-collar worker is the same for blacks and whites, once we control for other factors in the model in general and the race-specific effect of education in particular. One thing we learn in the comparison of results for Models 5 and 6 is that the net difference in expected INCOME between upper white-collar whites and blacks was partially attributable to the fact that attaining a higher level of education did not produce the same income dividend for blacks as it did for whites. Once we allow for this difference in the process of income determination (i.e., once we allow the increment to expected INCOME associated with additional schooling to be smaller for blacks than for whites), we provide one possible

48

explanation for why upper white-collar workers who were black had lower expected INCOME than upper white-collar workers who were white: Their additional education was valued at a lower rate of return. We do not invalidate the initial observation that upper white-collar blacks were at an income disadvantage relative to upper white-collar whites. Instead, the results from Model 6 suggest one mechanism involved in producing that disadvantage. In addition, we learn that, among skilled workers, what initially appeared as a racial difference in the effect of being skilled versus upper white-collar is, in part, a function of the differential returns to education that accrue to whites and blacks.

Separate Subgroup Regressions

Starting with an observed difference in expected INCOME between two groups—older black workers and older white workers—we have now worked through a series of models in which we added controls for occupation, education, and tenure. Further, we expanded the model specification to include tests for the differential effects of these additional variables for black and white workers. This last step may lead the reader to wonder why we chose to estimate a model such as Model 6 on the full sample (allowing the effects of all independent variables to differ by subgroup) rather than estimate separate regressions within subgroups. Why not simply split the sample into black workers and white workers, then estimate for each subgroup a model that predicts INCOME as a linear function of occupational category dummy variables, education and job tenure? In fact, these are equivalent approaches, *provided* one uses the appropriate statistical procedures for hypothesis testing and the standard OLS assumptions are met.

In developing the full-sample model with interaction effects, we noted six major points:

1. In the absence of specified product terms (interaction effects), the coefficients for independent variables reported "average" effects or, when other independent variables were included in the specification, "average" partial effects.

2. By expanding the specification to include product terms (thereby removing the constraint of equivalent effects across all groups), we could compare the R^2 values from the two specifications and determine whether relaxing the constraint of equal subgroup effects resulted in a significant improvement in the fit of the model: If the increment to R^2 resulting from the

inclusion of product terms was sufficiently large (in statistical terms), we could reject the null hypothesis that effects were equal across subgroups.

3. Once we estimated Model 6 on the full sample, we identified the t tests associated with the coefficients for OCC_2 through OCC_6 as tests of the net occupation effects for white workers and the t test associated with the coefficient for BLACK as a test of the net effect of being African American on expected INCOME for upper white-collar workers.

4. In order to test whether the effect of an independent variable was significant for the black workers, it was necessary to construct a t test for the sum of two coefficients.

5. In order to test whether the effects of two independent variables were significantly different from each other (e.g., to test whether operatives were different from service workers), it was necessary to construct a t test for the difference between two coefficients.

6. By examining the t tests for the product terms, we could determine whether the effects of explanatory variables differed by race.

By estimating separate regressions within the subgroups (e.g., one regression for black workers and a second regression for white workers), we automatically estimate group-specific effects. In other words, for each group we know whether a given independent variable has a significant effect, thereby obviating the need for the procedure outlined in point 4 above. However, if the purpose of estimating separate subgroup regressions is to assess the significance of group differences in effects, an actual test for the *difference* in effects is needed.

In the absence of an explicit test, researchers can fall into two traps. Imagine, for example, an analysis that predicts political activism as a function of age. Suppose we expected the relationship between age and political activism to differ by level of education; specifically, suppose we hypothesized that the relationship between age and political activism would differ for college graduates compared with those without college degrees. Suppose also that we have random samples of 500 respondents in each group. If separate regressions were estimated within these two educational groups, we might find an apparent "difference" between the estimated effects for age. For example, suppose the age effect for college graduates is estimated to be $-.16$ and the age effect for non-college graduates is $-.32$. Can we argue that the effect for college graduates is smaller than the effect for those with less formal schooling simply because the estimated coefficient for college graduates is half the size of the other? Most readers will recognize the risk in this statement. If the purpose of the research is to generalize from sample to population, it is always necessary to couple consideration of a point estimate with the error associated with that estimate. When evaluating the importance of the effect of an independent variable in a regression model, it is not simply the magnitude of the coefficient that matters, it is the magnitude of the coefficient relative to its standard error. The situation is the same when making statements about the relative magnitude of effects, that is, whether the effects are equal or unequal. The magnitude of the difference in coefficients must be evaluated relative to the standard error of the difference. In this case, then, we have too little information to be able to say anything about the relative effect of age on political activism for different educational groups.

With that in mind, let us suppose that, in addition to coefficient estimates, we know the standard errors of these estimates: The $-.16$ coefficient has a standard error of $.11$ and the coefficient of $-.32$ has a standard error of $.14$. With this additional information, we can see that the effect is not significant at conventional alpha levels for the college graduate group, but the coefficient is significant at the $.05$ level for the nondegree group.[10] With this additional information, can we now claim that the effect of age is stronger for the nondegree group than for the group with college degrees? Again, the answer is no. Although we may have established that age is a significant predictor of political activism in the nondegree group only, we have performed no inferential test for the *difference* in effects. If the research question asks whether the two effects are equal—that is, H_0: $\beta_{CG} - \beta_{NCG} = 0$ (where β_{CG} is the effect of age for college graduates and β_{NCG} is the effect for nongraduates)— then it is not the significance of B_{CG} or of B_{NCG} per se that is relevant to our null hypothesis of no difference in effect between groups. The appropriate estimate is $(B_{CG} - B_{NCG})$. The magnitude of this statistic must be evaluated relative to the standard error of $(B_{CG} - B_{NCG})$. Equation 4.5 provides a formula for this test when coefficient estimates are from a single equation. When coefficients are estimated from separate regressions, however, the definition of the test is somewhat different.[11]

To illustrate these issues, let us return to our earnings data. We can run separate subgroup regression for older white workers and older black workers and obtain the results reported in Table 4.7. Because the regression coefficients were estimated on separate samples, the estimated effects (the Bs) are necessarily uncorrelated; that is, the covariance of the estimates is zero. Therefore, it might seem that the formula for the standard error should reduce to the square root of the sum of the

TABLE 4.7
Results for Separate Subgroup Regressions

	Blacks	Whites
Constant	3,295.2	4,962.5
	(416.0)	(494.9)
OCC_2	−1,068.8	−2,155.4
	(411.2)	(319.8)
OCC_3	−718.4	−2,167.9
	(371.1)	(275.3)
OCC_4	−1,144.5	−3,132.1
	(354.9)	(305.2)
OCC_5	−1,605.1	−4,281.2
	(371.2)	(430.2)
OCC_6	−1,611.5	−3,851.3
	(371.3)	(466.6)
EDUC	186.3	359.1
	(19.7)	(33.3)
TENURE	94.5	80.3
	(6.9)	(8.6)
R^2	.31887	.24450
F	61.06	105.50
$RSS/(n - k - 1)$	4,046,652.4	18,754,709.2
N	921	2,290

NOTE: Regression coefficients with standard errors (in parentheses).

variances. However, the variances of these separate subgroup coefficients are based, in part, on separate subgroup estimates of the population variance. Each of the two estimates of the population variance is based on only "part" of the sample and therefore uses different pieces of the residual sum of squares. This means we must calculate a pooled estimate of the population variance that combines information from the two groups (Kmenta, 1986). Further, as the subgroups may be of different size (we have more than twice as many whites as blacks), this pooled estimate must weight each subgroup estimate by appropriate degrees of freedom (Long & Miethe, 1988).

Assuming equality of group variances (i.e., homogeneity of variance), the formula for the pooled estimate of the population variance is

$$s^2_{pooled} = \frac{(n_1 - k_1 - 1)s_1^2 + (n_2 - k_2 - 1)s_2^2}{N - (k_1 + k_2 + 2)}, \quad [4.6]$$

where n_1 and n_2 are the number of cases in the subgroups, $N = n_1 + n_2$, k_1 and k_2 are the number of independent variables included in each subgroup regression, and s_1^2 and s_2^2 are the mean residual sums of squares from their respective subgroup regressions.[12] The appropriate t test for the difference in coefficients from separate subgroup regressions is

$$t = \frac{B_1 - B_2}{s_{pooled}\left(\dfrac{s_{B_1}^2}{s_1^2} + \dfrac{s_{B_2}^2}{s_2^2}\right)^{1/2}}, \qquad [4.7]$$

where $s_{B_1}^2$ and $s_{B_2}^2$ are the variances of the estimates B_1 and B_2, and s_1^2 and s_2^2 are as before. By performing the above t test, we can reproduce the t test for the product (interaction) term in the full-sample regression model.

For example, using the results reported in Table 4.7, we can test whether the effect of education is the same for blacks and whites by substituting into Equations 4.6 and 4.7. Calculating the pooled estimate of the population variance, we have

$$s_{pooled}^2 = \frac{(921 - 8)(4,046,652) + (2,290 - 8)(18,754,709)}{3,211 - 16}$$

$$= 14,551,750.$$

Substituting into the t-test formula, we find

$$t = \frac{186.3 - 359.1}{3,814.7\left(\dfrac{386.8}{4,046,652} + \dfrac{1108.9}{18,754,709}\right)^{1/2}}$$

$$= \frac{-172.7}{47.5}$$

$$= -3.6.$$

A comparison of the numerator and denominator of this t statistic with the coefficient and standard error for BLEDUC as reported in Table 4.6 makes clear the equivalence of the two procedures.

However, in developing this equivalence we have simply substituted into the appropriate equations (Equations 4.6 and 4.7) without checking to see if the assumptions underlying this t test have been met. In fact, until now the entire discussion has neglected the question of whether the OLS assumptions have been met. While formulating a general understanding of the interpretation of coefficients for regressors involving binary-coded dummy variables, we have been proceeding as if the OLS assumptions were never problematic. It is time to correct that deficiency. Indeed, our current emphasis on inferential tests requires that we examine these assumptions more closely. In particular, given the nature of the present example, we need to test for homogeneity of variance (or homoscedasticity) before we draw *any* conclusions about differential effects from *either* the full sample *or* the separate subgroup regressions.

Although it is always important to test whether OLS assumptions have been met, a careful comparison of results reported in Table 4.7 to those reported in Table 4.6 strongly suggests that we have a problem. The significance tests for the net effects of occupation among blacks (based on the full sample estimation of Model 6) that were reported in Table 4.6 are *not* reproduced when separate subgroup regressions are estimated; the estimated regression coefficients are the same, but the standard errors are notably different. When separate subgroup regressions are estimated, the standard errors for blacks are smaller than those reported in Table 4.6, and the standard errors for whites are larger than those reported in Table 4.6. How can we account for this inconsistency?

Dealing With Heteroscedasticity

We have been developing models based on our underlying hypotheses that both the level of earnings and the structure of earnings determinants differ by race. In other words, we began by identifying a gross difference in the level of earnings for blacks and whites, and then proceeded to address the question of differential effects for explanatory variables such as the occupation dummy variables, education, and job tenure by specifying interaction terms. However, these tests are potentially problematic, because they assume that the variances of the two groups are the same.

Although the estimates of the regression coefficients obtained from Model 6 using the full sample are identical to those obtained from the estimation of separate subgroup regressions, the estimate of the population variance, RSS/$(N - k - 1)$, obtained from the full sample regression will approximate the pooled estimate derived from the separate subgroup regressions only if the assumption of homoscedasticity (equal subgroup variance) is met. When substituting into Equation 4.6, the difference in subgroup estimates of the population variance became evident. Mean residual sums of squares from the subgroup regression for blacks was 4,046,652; the comparable value for whites was 18,754,709. The full sample estimate from Model 6 (14,551,750) utilizes all observations. It is based on more information than either of the separate subgroup estimates, because each subgroup estimate uses only a portion of the observations (in this case, only the 921 blacks or the 2,290 whites). But this estimate from the full sample is an unbiased estimate of the population variance only if we can assume that the variance of u_i is constant across values of X_{ki} (i.e., in this case, across subgroups). Is the assumption that the variance of u_i does not differ by group valid in this case? To answer that question, we must look more closely at our results.

The assumption of homoscedasticity, or equal variance, states that the variance of the disturbance term conditional on particular values of the independent variables is a constant, σ^2. In research problems that involve the comparison of groups, testing for heteroscedasticity (the violation of the assumption) is necessary. Many tests for heteroscedasticity require that the researcher examine the squared residuals from an OLS estimation (the e_i^2). Basic statistical texts provide a more extensive discussion of this problem and of the testing procedures available (e.g., Gujarati, 1988; Johnston, 1984). This discussion will be limited to two tests and a discussion specific to our concerns.

In this example, we hypothesize that the size of the variance is a function of race, that is, that the variance is not equal across racial subgroups. A straightforward test would be to compare the mean residual sums of squares derived from the separate subgroup regressions for whites and blacks. If we have homogeneity of variance, then the error variance around the estimated regression planes should be equal for the two groups. We can thus posit as the null hypothesis that these variances are equal—that is, H_0: $\sigma_1^2 = \sigma_2^2$ —and use the mean residual sums of squares as our estimates of these parameters. If we construct a ratio of the larger variance to the smaller, then that ratio should equal 1 if the variances are equal; as the ratio departs from 1, the assumption of equal variances becomes less tenable. If u_i are assumed to be normally distributed and if the assumption of homoscedasticity is valid, the ratio of the variances follows the F distribution. Therefore, we can construct the following test statistic:

$$F_{n_1 - k_1 - 1, n_2 - k_2 - 1} = \frac{\text{RSS}_1/n_1 - k_1 - 1}{\text{RSS}_2/n_2 - k_2 - 1},$$ [4.8]

where the numerator is the larger of the two error variances from the separate subgroup regressions and the denominator is the comparable value from the group with the smaller variance. In this case, k_1 and k_2 (the number of independent variables included in each regression) will be the same, because the specification is the same. From the quantities reported in Table 4.7, we have

$$F_{913,2282} = 18,754,709.2/4,046,652.4 = 4.63.$$

For subgroups this large, an F value of 4.63 is significant at the .001 level, requiring us to reject the null hypothesis of equal variance (homoscedasticity) in favor of unequal subgroup variances (heteroscedasticity). The coefficient estimates from the full sample estimation of Model 6 are still unbiased; however, under heteroscedasticity t tests are inaccurate. Under conditions of heterogeneity of variance between subgroups, addressing the question of differential subgroup effects for explanatory variables is much more complicated, because the inferential tests for differences in effects are ambiguous: It is unclear whether the test results are caused by a difference in group effects, a difference in group variances, or both.

This general category of problem—testing the equality of normally distributed means when the variances are unequal—is known as the Behrens-Fisher problem (Amemiya, 1986, p. 36). A number of solutions have been proposed (e.g., Goldfeld & Quandt, 1978; Kendall & Stuart, 1979, p. 159; Welch, 1938). These solutions rely on either some sort of data transformation or reweighting scheme designed to negotiate the problem of unequal variance or a recalculation of the distribution of the test statistic to adjust for bias. In our example, however, the problem may be somewhat easier to solve.

Initially, we proceeded on the basis of a conventional regression specification, noted the possibility of alternative combinations of explanatory variables that could be hypothesized, but never questioned the functional specification of the relationships we would be testing. Although we have been using INCOME (measured as dollars earned from wages and salary) as the dependent variable, the actual functional specification we have employed may not be the most appropriate choice. For example, if wages are distributed log-normally (an assertion supported by a sizable body of literature in economics), then our problem of unequal variance may stem from an error in specification.

Interpreting Dummy Variables
in Semilogarithmic Equations

We routinely specify regression equations using the original metric of both the dependent and independent variables. In following this convention, we preserve the interpretation of regression coefficients with which readers are most familiar: change in the expected value of Y per unit change in X. Occasionally, however, the functional specification will call for a transformation of the independent variables, the dependent variable, or both. One of the most common transformations encountered in the research literature is the logarithmic transformation, a transformation that is particularly useful when the distributions of variables are highly skewed.[13] Though use of the log transformation is routinely suggested as a remedial measure for dealing with heteroscedasticity (Gujarati, 1988; Maddala, 1992), in this example, shifting to a natural logarithmic transformation of earnings is also consistent with a particular understanding of earnings distributions that argues that the difference in an earnings level of $5,000 versus $10,000 does not have the same meaning as a difference in an earnings level of $50,000 versus $55,000. In the original metric distribution of earnings, a difference of $5,000 carries the same meaning, regardless of where in the distribution the increment is calculated; it is always simply an increment of $5,000. In contrast, viewing the $5,000 increment in proportional terms, we see that increasing an income of $5,000 by an additional $5,000 represents an increment of 100%, whereas adding $5,000 to an earnings level of $50,000 represents an increment of only 10%. To produce a proportionately equivalent effect at $50,000, we would need to move to $100,000 (an increase of $50,000 or 100%). By using the logarithmic transformation of earnings, we specify the relationships between the independent variables and the dependent variables in proportional terms. In a semilogarithmic model, only the dependent variable or the independent variables are log transformed; in this example, we use the log transformation of the dependent variable, earnings, and leave the independent variables in their original metric. We can define a semilogarithmic model of Y as follows:

Model 7: $\ln(Y_i) = f(\text{race, occ, educ, tenure})$
$$= \beta_0 + \beta_1 \text{BLACK} + \beta_2 \text{OCC}_2 + \beta_3 \text{OCC}_3 + \beta_4 \text{OCC}_4$$
$$+ \beta_5 \text{OCC}_5 + \beta_6 \text{OCC}_6 + \beta_7 \text{EDUC}$$
$$+ \beta_8 \text{TENURE} + \beta_9 \text{BLOCC}_2 + \beta_{10} \text{BLOCC}_3$$
$$+ \beta_{11} \text{BLOCC}_4 + \beta_{12} \text{BLOCC}_5 + \beta_{13} \text{BLOCC}_6$$
$$+ \beta_{14} \text{BLEDUC} + \beta_{15} \text{BLTENURE} + u_i.$$

When X_{ki} is a continuous measure, we interpret the regression coefficient (e.g., β_8) as the relative change in Y for a given absolute change in X (e.g., the proportional change in INCOME for a one-year change in TENURE). If we multiply β_8 by 100, we then have the percentage change in INCOME for an absolute change in X. For example, if B_8 were .014, we would say that predicted Y changes 1.4% for each additional year of job tenure. Although this interpretation is valid when the independent variable is a continuous measure, Halvorsen and Palmquist (1980) have shown that it is *not* correct to interpret the coefficient of a dummy variable in this way.

Suppose X_{ki} were a dummy variable instead of a continuous variable. Because dummy variables utilize discrete codes (i.e., the values 0 and 1), we define no slope by the regression coefficient; therefore, we cannot represent the coefficient of a dummy variable as the derivative of the dependent variable with regard to the dummy variable. Further, because the coefficient for the dummy variable captures the difference in subgroup means between the designated group and the reference group (in units of the dependent variable), when $Y^* = \ln Y$, the coefficient for the dummy variable in the semilogarithmic specification (B_k) already expresses relative change in units of $\ln Y$. As Halvorsen and Palmquist (1980) have shown, the coefficient of a dummy variable in a semilogarithmic regression actually equals

$$B_1 = \ln \frac{1 + \hat{Y}_1 - \hat{Y}_{\text{ref}}}{\hat{Y}_{\text{ref}}}, \qquad [4.9]$$

where $\hat{Y}_1$ is the predicted value of $\hat{Y}$ for the group coded 1 and Y_{ref} is the predicted value of Y for the reference group. In order to find the percentage effect of the dummy variable on Y (measured in the original units of Y rather than relative to the log-transformed distribution), it is necessary to use the inverse of the logarithmic function (i.e., the exponential, or antilog, function). The percentage difference associated with being in the group coded 1 rather than in the reference group is then equal to

$$100[\exp(B_1) - 1]. \qquad [4.10]$$

Therefore, if the coefficient for a dummy variable (e.g., B_1, the coefficient for BLACK) is $-.632$, we would find the antilog of $-.632$ to the base e, which is .532, then subtract 1, for a value of $-.468$. The expected value of Y for the designated group (in this case, blacks) is .468 (46.8%) lower than the value for the reference group (in this case, whites).

Table 4.8 reports the results from the full sample estimation of Model 7 on the left; the right-hand columns report results from separate subgroup regressions for blacks and whites.

Our first task is to see if we now meet the assumption of homogeneity of variance. Substituting into Equation 4.8, we have

$$F_{913,2282} = .27774/.21983 = 1.263.$$

Given the computed F value, we fail to reject the null hypothesis of equal variances and can therefore proceed with our assessment of differential effects for blacks and whites.

Before summarizing the substantive results, let us compare findings from the two regression formats reported in Table 4.8. First, we see that the coefficient estimates from the two parts of the table are the same. Further, we see that the standard errors calculated within the different formats are very similar. Third, the inferential tests from the two formats lead us to the same substantive conclusions. For whites, holding an upper white-collar job provides a significant earnings advantage, even when education and job tenure are controlled. Both education and job tenure have significant positive net effects on expected earnings. For blacks, being an upper white-collar worker does not provide the same income advantage as it does for whites; in fact, controlling for other factors in the model, upper white-collar workers earn significantly more income than laborers, but remaining occupational differences are not significant. The net effect of education on INCOME does not differ for blacks and whites; however, the effect of job tenure is stronger for

TABLE 4.8
LN(INCOME) on Explanatory Variables With Full Set of Interactions

| | Full Sample Regression | | Separate Subgroup Regressions | |
	General Model	Blacks[a]	Whites	Blacks
Constant	8.353		8.353	7.720
	(.056)		(.054)	(.109)
BLACK	−.632			
	(.115)			
OCC$_2$	−.244	−.029	−.244	−.029
	(.036)	(.099)	(.035)	(.108)
OCC$_3$	−.174	.056	−.174	.056
	(.031)	(.090)	(.030)	(.097)
OCC$_4$	−.328	−.056	−.328	−.056
	(.035)	(.086)	(.033)	(.093)
OCC$_5$	−.585	−.105	−.585	−.105
	(.049)	(.090)	(.047)	(.097)
OCC$_6$	−.510	−.209	−.510	−.209
	(.053)	(.090)	(.051)	(.097)
EDUC	.049	.043	.049	.043
	(.004)	(.005)	(.004)	(.005)
TENURE	.014	.027	.014	.027
	(.001)	(.002)	(.001)	(.002)
BLOCC$_2$	.215			
	(.106)			
BLOCC$_3$	.230			
	(.095)			
BLOCC$_4$	.272			
	(.093)			
BLOCC$_5$	.480			
	(.102)			
BLOCC$_6$	.301			
	(.104)			
BLEDUC	−.006			
	(.006)			
BLTEN	.013			
	(.002)			
Mean RSS	.23654		.21983	.27774
R^2	.42489		.32987	.30082

NOTES: Regression coefficients with standard errors (in parentheses).
a. Entries for blacks were calculated by summing coefficients; standard errors were calculated as $[\text{var}(B_i) + \text{var}(B_j) + 2\,\text{cov}(B_i, B_j)]^{1/2}$.

blacks than for whites. The race-by-occupation interaction terms suggest that the net effect of occupation does differ by race: occupational differences in expected income are less pronounced among blacks. We can summarize these results by saying that the net effect of being black differs by occupation: Black upper white-collar workers are at a significant income disadvantage relative to white upper white-collar workers, and this advantage is maintained across all but one occupational category. Among service workers, the difference in expected income between blacks and whites (controlling for differences in education and job tenure) is not significant.[14]

Testing for Heteroscedasticity
With More Than Two Groups

A number of formal tests for heteroscedasticity are available. For example, the Goldfeld-Quandt test, appropriate when the number of observations is not large, is used fairly routinely; however, it also requires a division of observations into two groups (Goldfeld & Quandt, 1972; Gujarati, 1988). Another frequently cited detection procedure is proposed by Glejser (1969), who suggests estimating a series of regressions that specify $|e_i|$ as a function of each independent variable included in the model (for limitations, see, e.g., Gujarati, 1988; Maddala, 1992). In our example, we would calculate the e_i using results from Model 6 and then regress $|e_i|$ on BLACK. The F test for this equation indicates whether the hypothesis that errors are homoscedastic should be rejected. The extension from two groups to j groups requires that the $|e_i|$ be regressed on $j - 1$ dummy variables; the F test can again be examined to determine whether the hypothesis of constant variance across groups should be rejected.

Tests for heteroscedasticity are performed as diagnostics on already estimated regression models. Researchers interested in determining whether they are likely to encounter this problem may prefer to test for homogeneity of variance before initiating regression procedures. Recent comparative studies of commonly used homogeneity of variance tests indicate that there is considerable variation in the power and robustness of these tests (Conover, Johnson, & Johnson, 1981). A common limitation of these tests (e.g., Bartlett's, 1937) is their sensitivity to nonnormality. One of the tests that performed well in these comparative analyses was suggested by Levene (1960). As it happens, this test is similar in structure to Glejser's tests for heteroscedasticity. Levene suggests using one-way analysis of variance on the absolute value of deviation scores; the robustness of the test is improved when deviations around the median are substituted for deviations around the mean. To perform this test, the researcher must initially calculate $|Y_{ij} - \tilde{Y}_j|$, where $\tilde{Y}_j$ refers to the median value for group j. Because one-way analysis of variance is equivalent to performing a dummy variable regression with $j - 1$ dummy variables, we would then estimate the regression equation

$$|Y_{ij} - \tilde{Y}_j| = B_0 + B_1 D_1 + \ldots + B_{j-1} D_{j-1} + e_i$$

and examine the F test for the equation to determine whether the null hypothesis of homogeneity of variance should be rejected.

Methods for Making Multiple Comparisons With Nonindependent Tests

By describing methods by which we can assess all possible group differences, we have opened another topic worthy of some discussion—the problem of multiple comparisons. This problem is one of the issues of simultaneous statistical inference (Miller, 1966). In our context, the problem stems from making multiple group comparisons from a single set of estimates. The larger the number of comparisons we perform, the more likely at least one of the comparisons will yield a "significant" result. The proper way to generate significance tests for multiple comparisons continues to be a focus of considerable debate. Here, a brief review is provided of two methods of dealing with the issue—the Bonferroni method and Fisher's protected t method (Darlington, 1990, pp. 249-275).

In our example, we examined differences in expected income by occupational group. The specification of upper white-collar worker as the reference category meant that we would directly estimate five comparisons: Upper white-collar workers were compared with the remaining five categories of workers. However, we also introduced a t test that allowed us to test the difference between estimated regression coefficients. The number of possible comparisons is equal to $j(j - 1)$, where j represents the number of categories; however, when the order of the comparison is irrelevant, the number of possible comparisons is reduced by half. For our six occupational groups, we could thereby generate 15 possible pairwise comparisons. The techniques for addressing this issue depend on whether the possible comparisons can be considered independent. In this example, the comparison of upper white-collar to lower white-collar workers is not independent of the comparison of upper white-collar to skilled workers because the chance selection of particularly high-income upper white-collar workers would affect both comparisons. The comparisons of upper white-collar to lower white-collar workers and skilled workers to operatives are independent (or orthogonal) comparisons; however, the significance tests on these comparisons are not fully independent. Both comparisons use the same estimate of the population variance, $RSS/(N - k - 1)$, in the calculation of their standard errors; a chance fluctuation in this estimate will affect the t values for both tests.

Ryan (1960) developed an application of the Bonferroni inequality to nonindependent tests, proving that the Bonferroni formula provides a slightly conservative estimate of the corrected significance level for most sets of nonindependent tests. The purpose of the formula is to produce a level of significance that has been corrected for the fact that multiple comparisons are being made. The Bonferroni approach approximates a corrected significance level (CSL) by multiplying the number of results being tested (referred to as the Bonferroni Correction Factor, or BCF) by the p value (the probability level associated with the computed t value) for the most significant result. Therefore, if the most significant of 15 results yields a p value of .003, then the corrected significance level for this estimate is CSL = 15(.003) = .045, where 15 represents the BCF. If the object is then to assess the significance of the coefficient with the next smallest p value, we would multiply the p value of that coefficient by 14 rather than 15. This approach, referred to as *layering*, would continue until the first nonsignificant result was found.

Dunn (1961) has shown that for two-tailed tests, the expression $[1 - (1 - CSL)^{BCF}]$ provides an upper limit for the corrected significance level. However, whereas the Bonferroni estimate is sometimes too conservative, the Dunn alternative is sometimes too liberal. To get a better sense of the behavior of the Bonferroni formula, consider two extreme cases (Darlington, 1990). In the first case, two tests are correlated at −1. For example, if we perform two one-tailed tests on the regression coefficient B_k we would be testing two null hypotheses: that $\beta_k \geq 0$ and that $\beta_k \leq 0$. These tests are correlated at −1 because rejection of the first null hypothesis precludes rejection of the second. Using the

Bonferroni formula, we can say that the probability of being able to reject at least one of these null hypotheses at the .025 level is not greater than .05, that is, 2(.025). In this case, BCF(p value) is equal to the corrected significance level .05, that is, the significance associated with a single two-tailed test of the null hypothesis that $\beta_k = 0$. Therefore, under these circumstances, the Bonferroni formula is not conservative.

In contrast, consider the case in which tests are correlated at +1. If we have a j-category variable and compare the first group to all others one at a time, we generate $j - 1$ comparisons. This situation could occur if we had a j-category qualitative measure and had included $j - 1$ dummy variables in a regression model. If all nonreference groups have the same mean value and infinite sample sizes, then the t value for all comparisons with a reference group of finite size will be the same; rejection of the null hypothesis in one case necessarily implies rejection of the null hypotheses in all cases. In this situation, the corrected significance level is equal to the observed p value. Therefore, had we applied the Bonferroni formula, we would have overestimated the corrected significance level. The inaccuracy of the Bonferroni formula is therefore linked to the degree of correlation among tests. The higher the positive correlation among tests, the more severe the error.

Fisher's approach is much less conservative than the Bonferroni method. With this approach, the researcher performs an initial F test to test the composite null hypothesis that categories do not differ. If the F test is significant, the researcher can proceed with any and all comparisons, because the t tests involved in these comparisons are "protected" by the significance of the initial F test. In our discussion of results from the various models, our first step was to test the statistical significance of the increment to R^2 accomplished by including a set of dummy variables denoting a qualitative characteristic (e.g., the dummy variables for occupation) or a set of interaction terms (e.g., the race-by-occupation product variables). After establishing the statistical significance through the F test, we investigated other hypotheses. By following this procedure, we were adopting Fisher's approach to the issue of multiple comparisons.

5. ALTERNATIVE CODING SCHEMES FOR DUMMY VARIABLES

Although thus far the presentation of dummy variables has assumed binary coding and the designation of a single reference group, other methods of coding dummy variables are available. Two alternatives to binary coding are effects coding and contrast coding. Both methods require that we use $j - 1$ dummy variables to represent a j-category nominal variable, just as before.

Effects-Coded Dummy Variables

As mentioned in Chapter 2, some researchers prefer to define a middle category as reference group rather than one of the extreme categories of an ordinal distribution. The choice is often defended as a means of constructing group comparisons that mimic a contrast of designated categories to an "average" value for the overall sample. If one wants to contrast subgroups with a sample average, the interpretive structure associated with effects coding is usually more convenient than the interpretation based on binary coding.

To facilitate the comparison of dummy variables coded according to these alternative techniques with binary-coded dummy variables, we will continue with INCOME as the dependent variable and concentrate on race and occupation as the nominal variables. Table 5.1 provides examples of how we would utilize effects coding and contrast coding of dummy variables to capture the information of race and occupational category. The top panel describes five dummy variables that have been generated by effects coding. Upper white-collar workers has been retained as the reference group; however, whereas the reference group in binary-coded dummy variables is uniformly coded 0, the reference group in effects-coded dummy variables is always coded −1. The group contrast captured by each dummy variable is between the reference group and the group coded 1. In this example, E_1 contrasts upper white-collar and lower white-collar workers, E_2 contrasts upper white-collar with skilled workers, E_3 contrasts upper white-collar workers with operatives, and so on. When the groups being contrasted are equal in size, the zero-coded groups do not influence the comparison. However, when subgroup sizes are not equal (as is frequently the case), the effect of zero-coded groups is present, though minimal; in fact, the effect of the zero-coded groups increases as the mean value for all

TABLE 5.1
Effects Coding and Contrast Coding of Dummy Variables

Occupational Category	Effects Coding E_1	E_2	E_3	E_4	E_5
Upper white-collar	−1	−1	−1	−1	−1
Lower white-collar	1	0	0	0	0
Skilled	0	1	0	0	0
Operative	0	0	1	0	0
Service	0	0	0	1	0
Laborer	0	0	0	0	1
	Contrast Coding C_1	C_2	C_3	C_4	C_5
Upper white-collar	.5	1	0	0	0
Lower white-collar	.5	−1	0	0	0
Skilled	−.25	0	.5	1	0
Operative	−.25	0	.5	−1	0
Service	−.25	0	−.5	0	1
Laborer	−.25	0	−.5	0	−1

zero-coded observations departs from the sample mean (Cohen & Cohen, 1983).

Table 5.2 reports zero-order correlations, means, and standard deviations for the effects-coded dummy variables and income. In addition to the dummy variables for occupational category, a dummy variable for race, ERACE, is coded 1 if white, −1 if black. Whereas the mean values for binary-coded dummy variables were equivalent to the proportion of cases in the designated group (i.e., the category coded 1), the mean value for effects-coded dummy variables indicates the discrepancy in category ns between the reference group (coded −1) and the group coded 1. In fact, the mean value is simply $(n_j - n_{ref})/N$. For example, E_1 codes 644 upper white-collar workers −1; 337 lower white-collar workers 1; and the remainder of cases 0. Therefore, the mean value of E_1 is $(337 - 644)/3,211 = -.096$. The negative sign indicates that the reference group contains more observations than the group coded 1; the magnitude indicates the size of this discrepancy relative to total sample size. The set of mean values indicates that the number of upper white-collar workers exceeds the number of lower white-collar workers, service workers, and laborers; but the category of skilled craftsmen and that of operatives each contains more observations than the upper white-collar category.

TABLE 5.2
Means, Standard Deviations, and Correlations for Dummy Variables

	E_1	E_2	E_3	E_4	E_5	Income
	Effects Coded Dummy Variables					
ERACE	−.132	−.057	−.231	−.272	−.333	.313
	(.000)	(.001)	(.000)	(.000)	(.000)	(.000)
E_1		.563	.565	.662	.644	−.270
		(.000)	(.000)	(.000)	(.000)	(.000)
E_2			.444	.584	.560	−.242
			(.000)	(.000)	(.000)	(.000)
E_3				.586	.562	−.354
				(.000)	(.000)	(.000)
E_4					.660	−.403
					(.000)	(.000)
E_5						−.420
						(.000)
Mean	−.096	.052	.045	−.111	−.093	6,903.220
s.d.	(.544)	(.671)	(.666)	(.527)	(.547)	(4,629.954)

	C_1	C_2	C_3	C_4	C_5	Income
	Contrast Coded Dummy Variables					
CRACE	.271	.132	.172	.164	.088	.313
	(.000)	(.000)	(.000)	(.000)	(.000)	(.000)
C_1		.265	−.257	−.006	.027	.396
		(.000)	(.000)	(.358)	(.063)	(.000)
C_2			−.068	−.002	.007	.270
			(.000)	(.462)	(.343)	(.000)
C_3				.009	.068	.056
				(.310)	(.000)	(.001)
C_4					.000	.105
					(.491)	(.000)
C_5						.040
						(.012)
Mean	−.021	.096	.150	.007	−.018	6,903.220
s.d.	(.346)	(.544)	(.389)	(.706)	(.443)	(4,629.954)

NOTE: Correlation coefficients with probability values (in parenthesis).

The variance of an effects-coded dummy variable is a function of the relative frequency of the two groups being contrasted, or $p_j + p_{ref} - (p_j - p_{ref})^2$. Again, as illustration, the variance of E_1 is a function of the relative frequency of upper white-collar and lower white-collar workers, such that $s_{E1}^2 = .1050 + .2006 - (-.0956)^2 = .2965$ and $s_{E1} = .544$.

The correlation coefficients of E_1 through E_5 with INCOME suggest that the contrast is strongest (the means most divergent) for upper white-collar workers and laborers (i.e., variable E_5). However, because the sample is not evenly divided across occupational and racial categories, interpretation of zero-order correlations remains ambiguous. Zero-order correlations among the dummy variables themselves continue to indicate relative group size. A correlation of .50 among effects-coded dummy variables will occur only when all groups are the same size. A zero-order correlation coefficient larger than .50 (e.g., the correlations between E_1 and E_5 or E_1 and E_4) occurs when the reference group contains more cases than the other groups; when the reference group is small relative to the other groups (e.g., r_{E2E3}), the coefficient falls below .50.

REGRESSION RESULTS

Although the difference in coding schemes yields numerically different regression coefficients, the overall fit of the model (as indicated by the R^2) and the significance of the effects of race and occupational category dummy variables on INCOME (indicated by the F test for R^2 in Model 1 and the increment to R^2 test for Model 3 versus Model 1) reproduce results reported for Models 1 and 3 in Chapter 3. The different coding scheme affects the way the information is captured—the manner in which group differences are arrayed—but it does not effect the overall picture because the underlying structure of group differences remains unchanged from earlier estimations; we simply view it from a different angle.

Recall that in the case of binary-coded dummy variables the contrast between the reference group and the designated group was achieved only when other dummy variables in the set were controlled. In other words, the subgroup contrast existed only as a partial effect. The situation with effects-coded dummy variables is similar, though the nature of the contrast changes. Here, the partial regression coefficient for E_1, controlling for E_2 through E_5, produces a contrast between lower white-collar workers and all groups in the sample. That makes the quantity estimated by the partial regression coefficient the difference between the expected value of income for group j and the unweighted mean of the expected values for all subgroups, or

$$B_k = \overline{Y}_j - \sum \overline{Y}_j / j,$$

TABLE 5.3
Regression Results Using Alternative Coding Schemes

| | Effects Coding | | | Contrast Coding | |
	Model 1	Model 3		Model 2	Model 3
Constant	6,220.5	6,277.8		6,567.7	6,751.5
	(85.8)	(83.2)		(78.8)	(88.7)
Race	1,601.4	838.0			838.0
	(85.8)	(86.2)			(86.2)
E_1		853.5	C_1	5,247.6	6,443.8
		(196.9)		(223.4)	(260.3)
E_2		129.2	C_2	1,510.6	2,842.1
		(141.4)		(137.2)	(271.1)
E_3		−908.9	C_3	1,987.3	1,494.8
		(140.9)		(192.4)	(196.3)
E_4		−1,817.1	C_4	695.5	519.1
		(211.4)		(102.1)	(102.3)
E_5		−1,952.2	C_5	172.2	67.5
		(200.6)		(163.1)	(161.1)
R^2	.09792	.24624		.22400	.24624
F	348.3	174.4		185.0	174.4

NOTE: Regression coefficients with standard errors (in parentheses).

where j is the number of categories on the original nominal measure and the $\overline{Y}_j$ (subgroup means) are summed across all subgroups. The unweighted mean of all group means is also reported in the intercept, making it the reference point from which all subgroup differences are calculated.

The unweighted mean of means and the overall sample mean are different measures; whether they are indeed different numbers depends on the variability in group means relative to group size. The general sample mean can be considered a weighted mean of group means, because we can arrive at the sample mean by multiplying each group mean by the number of cases in that group, summing across all groups, and then dividing by total sample size. In calculating the unweighted mean of means, each group mean receives an equal "weight" (equal to 1) regardless of the number of cases in that group. One consequence is that group means based on a few cases and measured imprecisely are treated the same as more precisely estimated group means based on substantial group size; however, this difference in precision will be reflected in the standard errors of the coefficients. This procedure also makes the unstandardized regression coefficients independent of relative group size.

Consider the results from the first model reported in Table 5.3. The effects-coded race variable (ERACE) is the only independent variable specified; therefore, the intercept should be equal to the mean INCOME for blacks plus the mean INCOME for whites, divided by two. Using the values reported in Table 2.2, the reader can verify that this is the case. The value $B_{ERACE} = 1,601.4$ is the difference between expected INCOME for whites ($7,821) and the unweighted mean of means for blacks and whites, that is, the intercept.

Model 3 includes both ERACE and the occupation dummy variables in the specification; therefore, the regression coefficient for ERACE indicates that, once differences in INCOME by occupational category have been taken into account, there remains a positive income effect associated with being white. Similarly, controlling for black/white differences in INCOME, lower white-collar workers and skilled workers average higher earnings income than the expected value of income across groups, with the advantage for lower white-collar workers exceeding the advantage for skilled workers. Operatives, service workers, and laborers are below the average, with the INCOME disadvantage appearing greatest for service workers and laborers. With effects-coded dummy variables, the partial regression coefficients between INCOME and one of the dummy variables for occupation, controlling for all other occupational dummy variables, can therefore be interpreted as a measure of the "eccentricity" or the "uniqueness" of the specified group (Cohen & Cohen, 1983). By squaring the semipartial correlation coefficients, we assess the extent to which variation in INCOME is explained by the distinctiveness of particular categories.

As was the case in previous chapters, we calculate the predicted INCOME for each subgroup by multiplying the coefficient estimates associated with the dummy variables by the values received by members of that particular group. When dummy variables were binary coded, this procedure amounted to adding the coefficients for dummy variables designating a particular group and disregarding all coefficients for dummy variables on which zero codes had been assigned. With effects-coded dummy variables, recall that the reference category is coded −1 on all dummy variables within a set; for instance, upper white-collar workers were coded −1 on all the occupational dummy variables. Therefore, in order to calculate the predicted INCOME for a white upper white-collar worker, we have the following:

$$Y_{UWC} = 6,277.8 + 838(1) + 853.5(-1) + 129.2(-1) - 908.9(-1)$$
$$- 1,817.1(-1) - 1,952.2(-1) = 10,811.3.$$

Similarly, to calculate the expected INCOME for black upper white-collar workers, we would have essentially the same equation except the coefficient for ERACE (838) would be multiplied by −1, for a predicted INCOME value of 9,135.3. By comparing the predicted INCOME values generated from Model 3 in Table 5.3 with the predicted IN-COME values generated from Model 3 in Table 3.2, the reader can verify that the set of predicted values produced is the same, regardless of the coding scheme used for the dummy variables. Therefore, the major difference between effects-coded dummy variables and binary-coded dummy variables lies in the way the reference point is defined. Rather than assessing each group relative to a particular (and perhaps arbitrarily chosen) reference group, effects coding compares each group with the entire set of groups.

In spite of these apparent differences in interpretation, Suits (1983) demonstrates that it is possible to shift interpretive frameworks by adding a constant to estimated regression coefficients for binary-coded dummy variables, thereby expressing the deviations of all subgroups from an unweighted average across all subgroups. As an illustration, consider the simplest case in which INCOME is regressed on a binary-coded dummy variable for race—BLACK—yielding the results reported for Model 1 in Table 3.1:

$$Y_i = 7,821.9 - 3,202.9(\text{BLACK}) + e_i.$$

By adjusting the B_k reported above by a constant value, c, we can shift from the interpretation associated with binary-coded dummy variables (comparing each of the designated categories to the reference category) to an interpretation consistent with effects-coded dummy variables (comparing each category to the mean of the subgroup means). We determine the value of c such that $\sum(B_k + c) = 0$, where B_k refers to regression coefficients associated with binary-coded dummy variables; therefore, $c = -(\sum B_k)/j$, where j is the number of categories on the qualitative measure. In this example, c would equal $-(-3,202.9/2)$ = 1,601.45. By adding c to all the dummy variable coefficients and subtracting c from the constant, we obtain

$$Y_i = 6,220.45 - 1,601.45(\text{BLACK}) + 1,601.45(\text{WHITE}).$$

We can express a coefficient for WHITE even though the original specification treated this category as the reference category; we simply assume that the "effect" of WHITE in the original specification was set to zero.

When more than one qualitative variable is involved in the specification, the adjustment is determined within sets of dummy variables. For example, when INCOME is regressed on BLACK and the occupation dummy variables, we obtain

$$Y_i = 10,811.4 - 1,676(\text{BLACK}) - 2,842.1(\text{OCC}_2) - 3,566.4(\text{OCC}_3)$$
$$- 4,604.5(\text{OCC}_4) - 5,512.7(\text{OCC}_5) - 5,647.8(\text{OCC}_6) + e_i.$$

The value of c_{RACE} is determined as before; that is, $c_{\text{RACE}} = -(-1,676/2)$ = 838. The value for c_{OCC} is equal to $-[(-2,842.1) + (-3,566.4) + (-4,604.5) + (-5,512.7) + (-5,647.8)]/6 = 3,695.58$. We add c_{RACE} to the coefficients for the two categories on race (where the coefficient of WHITE from the original specification was set to zero), we add c_{OCC} to the coefficients for the six categories on occupation (where the coefficient for upper white-collar worker from the original specification was set to zero), and we subtract c_{RACE} and c_{OCC} from the constant. We can thereby express all the group effects relative to the unweighted average across subgroups as

$$Y_i = 6,277.8 - 838(\text{BLACK}) + 838(\text{WHITE}) + 3,695.6\,(\text{OCC}_1)$$
$$+ 853.5(\text{OCC}_2) + 129.18(\text{OCC}_3) - 908.9(\text{OCC}_4)$$
$$- 1,817.12(\text{OCC}_5) - 1,952.2(\text{OCC}_6) + e_i.$$

Contrast-Coded Dummy Variables

The bottom panel of Table 5.1 illustrates a set of contrast-coded dummy variables. Through contrast coding, the researcher can specify particular comparisons of interest, subject to three conditions: (a) Representation of the j-category nominal scale requires that $j - 1$ contrasts be specified, (b) the set of codes for any contrast-coded dummy variable must sum to zero, and (c) the codes for any two dummy variables must be orthogonal. A general rule of thumb for producing contrast codes requires that we initially organize the set of categories into two aggregated groups.

In this example, a distinction can be made between white-collar and blue-collar workers. C_1 defines this first contrast between all white-collar workers and all blue-collar workers. Because two white-collar categories are to be combined, each category is coded .5; similarly, because the blue-collar category combines four groups, each of these categories is coded $-.25$; the negative sign "contrasts" blue-collar to white-collar workers, whereas the .25 is a function of equally weighting four subgroups to produce the aggregate. The sum of these codes equals 1.

Remaining dummy variables define contrasts within this initial subdivision. C_2, for example, contrasts the two members of the white-collar category. Because each of these groups now stands alone, one group receives a code of 1; the second is coded -1. C_3 contrasts skilled craftsmen and operatives with service workers and laborers. The former two groups are coded .5; the latter two are coded $-.5$. C_4 then defines the contrast between skilled workers and operatives, and C_5 the contrast between service workers and laborers.[15] We can test the independence of this set of contrast codes by summing the products of successive pairs of codes. For example, summing the products of codes for C_1 and C_2, we have $(.5)(1) + (.5)(-1) + (-.25)(0) + (-.25)(0) + (-.25)(0) + (-.25)(0) = 0$.

The bottom panel of Table 5.2 reports zero-order correlations, means, and standard deviations for contrast-coded dummy variables defined in Table 5.1. The means and standard deviations of contrast-coded variables are also a function of relative group sizes, but because the coding scheme involves quantities less than 1, the relationship between these frequencies and the mean values makes interpretation less useful.

As in previous examples, this set of dummy variables displays non-zero correlations with other variables in the set, even though the codes used to define the contrasts were designed to be orthogonal. The condition that the codes be orthogonal is not the same as requiring that the variables themselves be orthogonal. The correlation among the contrast-coded dummy variables within a set is again a function of relative group size. Only if observations had been equally divided across all groups would the correlations be zero.[16]

Interpretation of the zero-order correlations between contrast-coded dummy variables and income is also somewhat ambiguous. For C_2, C_3, and C_4, the interpretation is essentially that of effects-coded dummy variables, because for these three variables the contrast is captured by codes of -1 for one group, $+1$ for a second group, and 0 for remaining groups. This coding operation is equivalent to the technique of effects coding with one exception: In contrast-coded dummy variables, the -1 code is not consistently applied to the same group. These correlations therefore measure the extent to which the difference in average INCOME for the two groups receiving -1 or $+1$ codes accounts for the variation in INCOME; however, when group ns are unequal, the zero-coded groups are also implied in this measure.

The interpretation of correlations involving dummy variables with only two codes (such as C_1) is more straightforward. Because C_1 codes white-collar workers .5 and blue-collar workers −.25, the squared zero-order correlation between income and C_1 measures the proportion of the variance in income that is explained by the distinction between white-collar workers and blue-collar workers. When other dummy variables are not held constant, the consequence of the coding scheme is to produce *weighted* means of subgroup means. For example, because upper and lower white-collar workers receive the same code, the value of mean INCOME for white-collar workers that is relevant to this zero-order relationship is the mean value of the aggregate, with subgroup membership ignored; in other words, the mean value for white-collar workers is constructed as the value of INCOME summed across all white-collar workers (upper and lower alike) and then divided by the total number of white-collar workers. In this sense, the zero-order correlation involves the weighted mean of similarly coded group means, because the value could be found by multiplying each subgroup mean by the number of cases in the subgroup, summing across subgroups, and dividing by the aggregate number of cases. However, it must be noted that this interpretation is appropriate only when one is dealing with zero-order correlations involving a contrast-coded dummy variable with only two possible values. The general conclusion we can draw is that, although contrast-coded dummy variables provide a useful alternative for summarizing regression results based on the entire set of variables, simple descriptive statistics involving these dummy variables taken one at a time are not particularly useful.

REGRESSION RESULTS

The results of the regression estimation for Models 2 and 3 are reported in the left-hand columns of Table 5.3. Model 1 estimates were not included because they are exactly the same as those reported for effects-coded dummy variables. Once again, the values for R^2 and its F test reported in Table 3.1 of Chapter 3 are reproduced, underscoring the general equivalence of the three approaches in the multiple regression analytic setting.

The partialing procedure involved in the regression estimation allows a more straightforward interpretation of coefficients than we found with the bivariate measures, although some additional calculation is still necessary. The interpretation of the intercept in this model is the same as in the model with effects-coded dummy variables; it is the unweighted mean of all subgroup means, and it again provides the reference point for assessing group effects. Each dummy variable specifies a contrast between two groups or sets of groups. The partial regression coefficient associated with that variable is a function of the difference between unweighted means of means and the codes used to construct the contrast; groups receiving zero codes are excluded from the comparison because of the partialing procedure.

Specifically, the group contrast (C_j) is defined as

$$C_j = B \frac{n_{g1} + n_{g2}}{(n_{g1})(n_{g2})}, \qquad [5.1]$$

where n_{g1} is the number of groups included in the first subset, n_{g2} is the number of groups in the second subset, and B is the regression coefficient for the dummy variable. For example, the coefficient for C_1 is a function of the contrast between white-collar workers and blue-collar workers. Substituting into Equation 5.1, we have

$$C_1 = 5,247.6 \frac{2+4}{(2)(4)} = 5,247.6(.75) = 3,935.7.$$

Remaining contrasts can be calculated as follows:

$$C_2 = 1,510.6 \ (2) = 3,021.2$$

$$C_3 = 1,987.3 \ (1) = 1,987.3$$

$$C_4 = 695.5 \ (2) = 1,391.0$$

$$C_5 = 172.2 \ (2) = 344.4$$

Using the group means reported in Table 2.2, the reader can verify that each contrast does indeed reproduce the differences in group means or unweighted means of group means.

The standard errors for the contrasts can be found by multiplying the standard error for the coefficient by the same factor we used to weight the coefficient itself. For example, the standard error for the contrast of upper white-collar workers to lower white-collar workers (C_2) is $(137.2)(2) = 274.4$. This value is the same as the value reported for OCC_2 in Model 2 of Table 3.1. The t tests associated with these coefficients allow us to evaluate whether the contrasts defined by the dummy variable generalize to the population. In Model 2, for example, the coefficients for C_1 through C_4 are all significant at better than the .001 level, but the coefficient for C_5 is not. We conclude that, in the population, the unweighted average income for upper white-collar and lower white-collar workers is higher than the unweighted mean of blue-collar groups; upper white-collar workers average higher income than lower white-collar workers; the unweighted average for skilled workers and operatives exceeds that of service workers and laborers; and skilled workers average higher incomes than operatives; but predicted income for laborers is not significantly different from the predicted income for service workers.[17]

When all other dummy variables are controlled, the squared semipartial correlation coefficients report the proportion of sample variance in Y explained by a particular contrast. The semipartials reported for Model 2 in Table 5.3, for example, indicate that the largest proportion of variance is accounted for by the contrast between white-collar and blue-collar workers (i.e., $.365^2 = 13.3\%$). However, summing the squared semipartial correlation coefficients will not produce the R^2 for the equation because the C variables were themselves intercorrelated. Only when all groups are equal in size will the contrast-coded dummy variables be uncorrelated, and only when regressors are orthogonal will the sum of the squared semipartial correlation coefficients equal R^2.

6. SPECIAL TOPICS IN
THE USE OF DUMMY VARIABLES

Up to this point, we have been working with the same set of variables from a single data set to investigate the interpretation of dummy variables within increasingly complicated specifications in order to illustrate the modeling flexibility that can accompany the use of dummy variables. In addition to the types of hypotheses already outlined, dummy variables have frequently been used in a variety of other formats. In this chapter we will explore some additional ways to utilize dummy variables in regression analysis.

Dummy Variables in Logit Models

Researchers dealing with binary or polytomous dependent variables have increasingly turned to logistic regression models. Because so many research questions involve group differences, logistic regressions with dummy variable regressors have also become common. Suppose, for example, our dependent variable of interest is mortality and our dummy independent variable is gender. The regression coefficient for a dummy variable in a logit regression represents a gender-dependent increment or decrement to the log-odds of dying. However, interpreting a log-odds metric is not as intuitively appealing as interpreting a simple odds ratio. Is it possible to shift from one framework to another? Yes; by taking the antilog of the logit coefficients, we accomplish an arithmetic translation of the additive effects (specified in the linear additive model predicting the log-odds) to multiplicative effects (in which the dependent variable is a simple odds ratio) (Alba, 1988). The shift from additive to multiplicative accompanies the shift from the log-odds to the odds ratio itself, because the logarithmic transformation allows us to represent multiplicative relationships as additive.

' To illustrate this technique, we will consider results from a model predicting mortality among older women as a function of self-assessed health and health risk factors, as reported by Idler and Kasl (1991). The dependent variable is the log-odds of dying during the 4-year period; the dependent variable, mortality, is coded 1 if the respondent died and 0 if the respondent survived. Subjective health status is treated as a set of three dummy variables, with "excellent health" serving as a reference group. Health status controls include cancer, diabetes, intermittent claudication, and hypertension (each coded 1, if present), the number of activities requiring help, the number of ADLs (activities for daily living that the respondent cannot perform without assistance), an index of body mass, age, and two dummy variables for being a present or past smoker, with nonsmokers serving as the reference group. Results from the logistic regression estimation are reported in Table 6.1; the antilogs of the logit coefficients for dummy variables are included in the right-hand column. Being in poor rather than excellent health increases the log-odds of dying, controlling for other variables in the model. Alternatively, we can say that the odds of dying during the study period are 3.12 times higher for women in poor health compared with women in excellent health, other things being equal. Similarly, controlling for other factors, the odds of dying for women in fair health are 2.85 times

TABLE 6.1

Dummy Variables in Logistic Regression

	Logistic Regression Coefficients (B)	Antilog (B)
Constant	−6.308***	
Self-assessed health		
poor (versus excellent)	1.138*	3.12
fair (versus excellent)	1.047*	2.85
good (versus excellent)	0.862*	2.37
Diabetes	0.963***	2.62
ADL score	0.041	
Activities	0.393*	
Intermittent claudication	0.982	2.67
Hypertension	0.369	1.45
Age	0.061**	
Current smoker (versus not)	0.769***	2.16
Past smoker (versus not)	−0.312	.73
Weight (kg)/height^2 (m)	−0.076***	

SOURCE: Adapted from Idler and Kasl (1991).
NOTE: *Coefficient significant at the .05 alpha level; **coefficient significant at the .01 alpha level; ***coefficient significant at the .001 alpha level.

higher, and for women in good health 2.37 times higher than the odds experienced by women in excellent health. Further, the net effects of smoking indicate that women who currently smoke face odds 2.16 times those of nonsmoking women. For sample members, the odds of dying for women who smoked in the past and then stopped are lower than the odds experienced by nonsmokers (.73 times their risk), but the estimated difference is nonsignificant.

The interpretation of coefficients for dummy variables in models where the dependent variable is logged has now been discussed in two places. In the first (the latter part of Chapter 4), the arithmetic translation of the coefficients allowed the reader to make an interpretation of proportional (or percentage) difference. In this chapter, we develop an interpretation of multiplicative effects. On the surface, the interpretation suggested for the coefficients associated with dummy variables in the semilogarithmic models developed in Chapter 4 may appear different from the interpretation developed for logit models. On the contrary, these two interpretations are only slight variations on a common procedure. In Equation 4.10, we defined the relative effect as the percentage difference associated with the presence of a characteristic (indicated by a code of 1 on the dummy variable): For example, among whites, the expected earnings for laborers were 40% less than the expected earnings for upper white-collar workers (controlling for other variables in the model). However, if we choose not to subtract 1 from the antilog of the coefficient, we simply present the complementary view of this occupational difference in multiplicative terms: laborers earn only 60% of what upper white-collar workers earn. Either way, the importance of using the antilog transformation of estimated regression coefficients associated with dummy variables to express relative effects remains the key.

Testing for Curvilinearity

Dummy variables are commonly used to designate categories of nominally coded independent variables. But we can also use dummy variables to represent segments of the distribution of ordinal or interval independent variables. For instance, if we suspect the presence of a nonmonotonic or curvilinear relationship between dependent and independent variables but have no good basis for predicting the particular form of curvilinearity, dummy variable regression provides a useful alternative to polynomial regression or the use of transformations. By representing a quantitative independent variable with a series of dummy variables, we cut the overall distribution into smaller pieces and then test to see if the effects across the series of dummy variables suggest a linear or a curvilinear relationship.

As an example using variables with which we are already familiar, consider the relationship between income and education. Rather than assuming that the effects of education are the same across the entire range, we may speculate that the increment to earnings associated with additional education depends on where in the overall distribution the effect of an additional year of schooling is assessed. In order to test for a curvilinear relationship between earnings and education, we would estimate two models:

Model 6.1: $Y = f(\text{years of schooling}) = \beta_0 + \beta_1 \text{EDUC} + u_i$

Model 6.2: $Y = f(\text{dummy variables for each grade completed})$
$$= \beta_0^* + \sum \beta_j \text{ED}_j$$

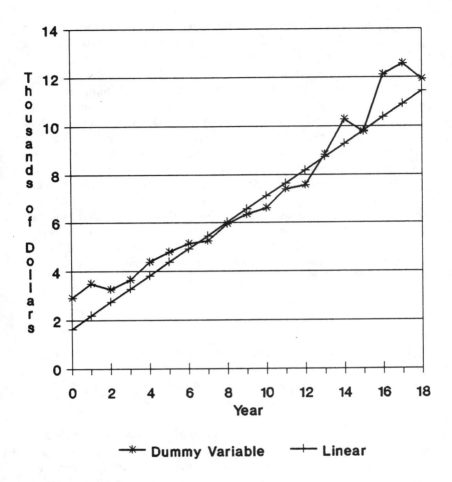

Figure 6.1. Test for Curvilinearity

In Model 6.1, education is entered as a quantitative independent variable (EDUC). In Model 6.2, education is specified as a series of dummy variables, denoted ED_j, where ED_0 is coded 1 if the respondent had no formal schooling, ED_1 is coded 1 if the respondent completed up to 1 year of schooling, and so on to ED_{17}, which is coded 1 if the respondent completed 17 years of formal schooling; the reference category designates 18 years of formal schooling.

Figure 6.1 illustrates results for these two models. A quick look at the graph suggests that the relationship may be slightly curvilinear. The differences in predicted earnings between successive groups are not uniform across the range of education. The slope is shallower at low levels of education, and appears somewhat steeper at higher levels of education, especially after 12 years of schooling. The model with dummy variables also explains slightly more variation in income than the model with linear specification. Model 6.1 explains 19.6% of the variance in earned income, whereas Model 6.2 explains 21.4% of the variance. Testing whether the increment to explained variance accomplished by relaxing the linearity assumption is statistically significant requires an F test of the following form (where the numerator degrees of freedom for F are determined by the number of additional independent variables in the dummy variable model, and the denominator degrees of freedom are equal to the number of cases reduced by the number of parameters estimated in the dummy variable model):

$$F = \frac{(R_2^2 - R_1^2)/(\text{df}_2 - \text{df}_1)}{(1 - R_2^2)/(N - \text{df}_2)} . \qquad [6.1]$$

Applying this F test to the results for Models 6.1 and 6.2, we have

$$F_{17, 3192} = \frac{(.21390 - .19624)/(19 - 2)}{(1 - .21390)/3,192} = \frac{.00104}{.00025} = 4.16,$$

which is statistically significant when compared with a critical F value of 2.65 at the .01 level.

If the independent variable is truly continuous in measurement, the original variable must be recoded into discrete categories before it can be represented as a series of dummy variables. When this is necessary, the second model is somewhat different from the one noted in the text in that the original (quantitative) independent variable is included in the specification along with the set of dummy variables. However, the formula for the F test comparing the R^2 from the two equations remains the same.

Piecewise Linear Regression

Dummy variables can also allow us to model an abrupt shift in the slope of a regression line. When the change in slope is gradual—that is, when the relationship between Y_i and X_{1i} increases or decreases in a linear fashion with values on X_{2i}—we can specify a product interaction term to capture this moderating effect. When the shift in slope is abrupt, however, we can use a dummy variable to help estimate the magnitude and significance of this shift. One research situation in which this technique is useful occurs when we can identify a threshold value in the distribution of our quantitative independent variable (X_i), and we expect the relationship between X_i and Y_i to differ on either side of that threshold value. For example, salespeople in retail trade often receive partial compensation from commissions that are graduated relative to the volume of merchandise they sell. Similarly, the relationship between output and cost may depend on economies of scale that modify the cost function at certain levels of output. Consider this latter context for purposes of illustration.

Suppose we have two distributions: The first distribution reports total output; the second reports total cost of production. Suppose further that we expect the cost per unit to drop when volume reaches 5,000. The value 5,000 therefore represents our threshold value, X^*. In order to estimate the shift in slope (cost per unit) that occurs at $X^* = 5,000$, we first calculate the deviations of each output level from the threshold value as $(X_i - X^*)$. Then we define a dummy variable (D_i) equal to 1 if output exceeds the threshold of 5,000 and 0 otherwise. The model then becomes

$$\text{Model 6.3: } Y_i = B_0 + B_1 X_i + B_2(X_i - X^*)D_i + e_i,$$

where B_1 estimates the slope for output levels less than 5,000 and ($B_1 + B_2$) estimates the slope beyond output levels of 5,000. B_2 therefore provides an estimate of the shift in slope and the t test associated with B_2 provides an inferential assessment of the significance of the estimated shift.

To continue with our example, when we regress total cost on output, we obtain the following results:

$$Y_i = 143.798 + .109 \text{OUTPUT} + e_i.$$
$$(27.455) \quad (.006)$$

This equation explains 93.75% of the variance in Y_i and suggests that, as output increases 1 unit, total cost increase about 11 cents. In other words, the marginal cost per item is 10.9 cents. When we estimate a piecewise regression model we find the following:

$$Y_i = 87.059 + .129\text{OUTPUT} - .045(\text{OUTPUT} - \text{OUTPUT}^*)(D_i) + e_i.$$
$$(34.264) \quad (.010) \qquad\qquad (.018)$$

This equation explains 95% of the variance in total cost, a significant increment of 1.25% over the previous model. In addition, we learn that at output levels below 5,000, the marginal cost per unit is almost 13 cents; however, at volume above 5,000, the marginal unit cost drops to 8.4 cents (.129 − .045).

Dummy Variables in Time-Series Data

When data are cross-sectional, dummy variables provide a method of estimating subgroup differences in the expected value of a dependent variable. Under these circumstances, subgroups can be defined by characteristics that we expect to be structurally related to the distribution of the dependent variable. When data are arrayed in a time series, dummy variables also allow us to group observations into categories; however, in time-series data, the grouping is more likely to be defined relative to key events. In time-series data, as in cross-sectional data, dummy variables frequently serve as proxies for distributional mechanisms that are difficult to measure and complicated to specify. Because they are proxies, the interpretation of the mechanisms behind the apparent difference is open to argument; but then the validity and interpretation of any model specification can be a source a disagreement.

Dummy variables can be used in time-series regressions to capture regional or subgroup differences. However, they can also be used to test the structural stability of parameters and to construct seasonal indexes. For example, researchers studying the growth in union membership in the United States frequently view passage of the Wagner Act as central to the development of unionism; investigations of the growth in military expenditures find it necessary to adjust for the effects of war mobilization; studies that attempt to model changes in the profitability of certain investments may want to specify shifts in tax law as determining factors. The impact of a key event can lead to a shift in the trend line as well as a restructuring of the process.

As an example of the former, consider Carl Chen's (1984) investigation of the impact of the Three Mile Island nuclear accident on the stability of the market model. His data consisted of weekly prices of 70 utility stocks for the first quarter of 1978 to the first quarter of 1980. Because the stocks of nuclear companies declined sharply after the incident, Chen wanted to test the stability of the market model by comparing parameter estimates before versus after the accident. He specified the following model:

$$\text{Model 6.4: } r_{jt} = \beta_{j0} + \beta_{j1}r_{mt} + u_{jt},$$

where r_{jt} is the weekly return on stock j at time t, r_{mt} is the market return proxied by the Standard and Poor's Index, and u_{jt} is the random disturbance term.

The dummy variable technique for testing the stability of the intercept (β_{j0}) and the slope (β_{j1}) requires that we divide the sample into two subsample periods. In this case, we define a dummy variable, $D = 0$, for observations taken before the accident and set $D = 1$ for observations taken after the accident (the week of the accident is omitted from observation). The test model then becomes

$$\text{Model 6.5: } r_j = \beta_{j0}^* + \beta_{j1}^* r_m + \beta_{j2}^* D + \beta_{j3}^* r_m D + u_j,$$

where β_{j2} estimates the difference in intercept values between the two periods and β_{j3} estimates the difference in the slope coefficient between the two periods. Chen's results for the subgroup of nuclear companies (those with more than a 10% nuclear fuel mix by 1980) are as follows (t values in parentheses):

$$r_j = -.0022 - .0031D + .3553r_m + .0614r_m D.$$
$$\quad\;\; (1.43) \quad (1.32) \quad (4.13) \quad\quad (.50)$$

On the basis of these results, the null hypothesis of no structural change cannot be rejected.

Dummy Variables and Autocorrelation

Consider a simple time-series model that predicts Y_t as a function of X_t and a dummy variable, D (coded 1 to indicate the later of the two periods), designed to estimate a process that spans two historical periods. A researcher interested in estimating both a shift in the level of Y

and a shift in the process generating Y would want to estimate the following model:

$$Y_t = B_0 + B_1 D + B_2 X_t + B_3 DX_t + e_t,$$

where B_1 estimates the shift in the level from period 1 to period 2, B_2 estimates the effect of X during the first period, and B_3 estimates the difference in the effect of X on Y between the second and first periods.

When estimating time-series regressions, the researcher must be concerned about violating the assumption of no autocorrelation. If an examination of residuals suggests that errors are correlated, OLS estimators are inefficient. In dealing with the problem of autocorrelation, researchers often assume that the disturbances are generated by first-order autoregressive process, that is, that the disturbance of the current time period is a linear function of the disturbance in the previous time period. The interdependence is measured by the coefficient of autocorrelation, rho. Remedial action then involves estimating a generalized difference equation in which $(Y_t - \rho Y_{t-1})$ is regressed on $(X_t - \rho X_{t-1})$, where ρ is an estimate of the coefficient of autocorrelation. But what about the dummy variables? Should the same transformation be applied to them? The answer is no (see Maddala, 1992, pp. 321-322). Given that the dummy variable defines two groups of observations, the pivotal observation is the first observation in the second period. The researcher must define the observations within those groups as follows:

1. Values on D remain 0 for all observations in the first period; the value for the first observation in the second period is $1/(1 - \rho)$; all other observations in the second period are set equal to 1.
2. The value of the product term, DX_t, is set to 0 for all observations in the first period; the first observation in the second period is set to X_t; remaining observations in the second period are set to $(X_t - \rho X_{t-1})$.

7. CONCLUSIONS

Although students sometimes regard the appellation *dummy variables* as humorously deprecating, the proper use of dummy variables can greatly enhance the flexibility of the regression model. However, proper use and interpretation of dummy variables does involve a number of complexities; the goal of this text has been to work through some of these complexities and provide readers with some guidelines for using dummy variables in their investigations. This treatment is by no means exhaustive. We have confined our attention to dummy variables as independent variables in single-equation models. However, methods for using binary variables in factor analysis, as endogenous or exogenous variables in structural equation systems, or as dependent variables in single- or multiple-equation systems receive an increasing amount of attention in the technical literature. Readers interested in pursuing more advanced topics dealing with the analysis of qualitative data are referred to Maddala's (1983) treatment of limited dependent variables in regression models; Haberman's (1978, 1979) two-volume work and Goodman's (1978) text on the analysis of qualitative data; Aldrich and Nelson's (1984) introduction to linear probability, logit, and probit models; Allison's (1984) discussion of event history models; Muthen's (1984) and Shockey's (1988) discussions of discrete data models with unobserved variables; the work by Clogg and Goodman (1984, 1985) on latent structure analysis; and Winship and Mare's (1983, 1984) papers on structural equation models and regression models with discrete data.

NOTES

1. To ensure a sufficient number of blacks to produce separate reliable estimates, households in predominantly black enumeration districts were oversampled. To simplify presentation, however, unweighted data are used in these exercises.

2. Of less practical importance are the remaining correlation coefficients among the dummy variables for occupational category. Because they reference different and mutually exclusive categories of a single attribute (occupation), these dummy variables are necessarily inversely related; that is, the correlations are negative. In the case of dichotomous variables, such as race in this example, the correlation between BLACK and WHITE (a dummy coded 1 if white) is necessarily -1.00. In the case of polytomous variables, however, the correlation, though still necessarily negative, will be less than perfect. A respondent who is a service worker is necessarily *not* a lower white-collar worker, a craftsman, an operative, or a laborer, but a respondent who is not a service worker may or may not be an operative, may or may not be a laborer, and so on. The size of the correlation between two dummy variables is a function of the number of cases coded 1 on each of the two variables and sample size. Thus in Table 2.3, craftsmen and operatives contain the largest number of cases, and the correlation between these two categories is also highest at $-.328$. In contrast, service workers and laborers are among the smallest

categories, with a correlation of $-.108$. In this situation, the correlation between the two dummy variables is equal to $-[(p_j p_{j'})/(1 - p_j)(1 - p_{j'})]^{1/2}$.

3. It is important to keep in mind that correlation coefficients are sensitive to the variances of the variables. For dummy variables, correlation coefficients depend on the relative frequencies of the various categories.

4. Because Model 1 is a bivariate regression, the F test and t test are equivalent tests: the t value for this test, -18.7, is the square root of the F value, 348.3. The information obtained through estimation of this regression model is also equivalent to the results from a one-way analysis of variance. Identical estimates of group means occur, and the F tests yield the same result (as well as the same numerical value). In addition, eta-squared (which in this example equals $.09792$) is the same as the R^2 for Model 1.

5. The degrees of freedom for the F test combine the degrees of freedom associated with the regression and residual sums of squares. Degrees of freedom for regression sums of squares are equal to the number of independent variables specified in the model (in this case 5 for the 5 dummy variables included). Degrees of freedom for residual sums of squares are equal to $N - k - 1$, where N is the number of observations and k is the number of independent variables in the model. When the F test is calculated as the ratio of R^2 to $1 - R^2$, the degrees of freedom are the same as those described above.

6. Because the choice of reference group is arbitrary from a mathematical standpoint, the researcher can always choose a different reference group and run the regression again, allowing the program to provide the t tests of interest.

7. Equation 4.4 also establishes that for blacks the difference in expected INCOME between occupational categories is captured by the sum of two coefficients.

8. In fact, the absence of significant occupational differences in average earnings for blacks is largely due to the additional control variables—education and job tenure. Had we estimated a model that included only race, occupation, and race/occupation product terms, the result would have been the following equation: $E(Y_i) = 10,960.3 - 3,958.4(BLACK) - 2,898.9(OCC_2) - 3,625.6(OCC_3) - 4,875.0(OCC_4) - 6,154.7(OCC_5) - 6,182.9(OCC_6) + 1,747.8(BLOCC_2) + 1,781.6(BLOCC_3) + 2,594.5(BLOCC_4) + 3,238.6(BLOCC_5) + 2,885.4(BLOCC_6)$. The t values associated with all coefficients were greater than ± 2.00. Using Equation 4.5 to construct comparable t tests for occupational differences in mean income among blacks, only the contrast between lower white-collar and upper white-collar workers failed to achieve significance at the $.05$ level. The reader can also use the estimates reported above to verify the equivalence of this specification with the calculation of race-by-occupation category means (as reported in Table 2.2).

9. It is possible to raise this question of differential effects for education and job tenure relative to occupational category as well. In this example, we have been interested in assessing differences between blacks and whites—not only in the level of expected income, but in the structure of effects that are linked to those income levels. Rather than speculate that the effect of education may differ by race, however, we could have hypothesized that it differed by occupational category. Perhaps additional years with the same employer, as an indicator of stability, loyalty to the firm, or accumulated job-specific training, pays a higher dividend for skilled craftsmen than it does for laborers. Perhaps additional years of formal education allow professional workers to command higher salaries, but do little to enhance the bargaining position of factory operatives. Had our interest been in occupation-specific effects of education and job tenure, the product terms would have numbered 10—1 for each occupational dummy variable and education; 1 for each occupational dummy variable and job tenure. If we tested only for occupational

differences in effects and found that significantly different effects were indicated for both education and job tenure, we would have constructed 6 pairs of parallel lines: to show the differential effect of education, each pair of solid lines for a specific occupational group would have the same slope for blacks and for whites, but a different slope from solid lines for other occupational categories. The same would hold true for the broken lines as illustration of the differential effects of job tenure.

10. Against a null hypotheses that $\beta = 0$, the t test for $-.16$ yields a t value of -1.45, and the t test for $-.32$ yields a t value of -2.29.

11. Tests for the equality (constancy) of parameters between two populations have been proposed. One such test adapts an analysis of variance framework (Chow, 1960; Maddala, 1992). The procedure requires that we first estimate the regression model for each group separately and obtain the residual sum of squares (RSS_j) from the separate regressions. We must also estimate the regression model for the pooled sample and obtain the RSS for the pooled regression. The F test (with $k + 1$ and $n_1 + n_2 - 2k - 2$ degrees of freedom) for the equality of parameters is $F = [(RSS_{pooled} - \sum RSS_j)/(k + 1)]/[\sum RSS_j/(n_1 + n_2 - 2k - 2)]$, where $\sum RSS_j$ is the sum of the RSS from the separate subgroup regressions, k is the number of independent variables in the model, and n_1 and n_2 are the number of observations in the two subgroups. An F value sufficiently large to reject the hypothesis of equality of parameters simply means that not all the independent variables have uniform effects across the two subgroups; however, this test does not indicate which parameters are different.

12. The mean residual sum of squares, $RSS/(n - k - 1)$, where n is the number of cases, k is the number of independent variables in the model, and RSS is the residual sum of squares calculated as $\sum e_i^2$, is routinely available through regression packages. Under OLS assumptions, this quantity provides an unbiased estimate of σ^2, the population variance of u_i.

13. In calculating logarithms, we must specify a base number. The most common bases are e, also known as the base for the "natural" logarithm, and 10. The value of e is 2.72. To take the logarithm of X to the base e, we determine the power to which e must be raised in order to produce X. Similarly, to take the logarithm of X to the base 10, we determine the power to which 10 must be raised in order to produce X. Logarithms collapse a distribution differentially. The nonlinearity is also clear, because the differences among $\log_{10}$ values of 1, 2, and 3 coincide with values in the original distribution of 10, 100, and 1,000.

14. The procedure for assessing the significance of the effect of being black for each occupational group is equivalent to the procedure developed for determining the significance of occupational differences for blacks versus whites. The effect of being black for upper white-collar workers is captured by the regression coefficient for BLACK. The effect of being black for lower white-collar workers equals $B_1 + B_9$; for skilled workers, it is $B_1 + B_{10}$; for operatives, $B_1 + B_{11}$; for service workers, $B_1 + B_{12}$; and for laborers, $B_1 + B_{13}$. To see if there are significant racial differences (net of other specified effects) within occupational categories, we use the t test described in Equation 4.5. Calculated t values for the five occupation groups described above are -4.07, -5.58, -5.63, -1.90, and -4.70, respectively.

15. There are a variety of choices to be made when creating contrast-coded dummy variables; in this situation, for example, we could have contrasted skilled workers to the combination of operatives, service workers, and laborers; skilled workers would have received a code of 1, whereas operatives, service workers, and laborers would have all

88

been coded $-\frac{1}{3}$. Remaining dummy variables would have contrasted operatives to the combination of service workers and laborers, with the final contrast being the same as the illustration in the text.

16. Readers familiar with traditional analysis of variance designs may note the similarity between this situation and the requirement of equal cell sizes to produce orthogonal designs in an n-way ANOVA.

17. An alternative test for the significance of the contrast defined by C_5, the difference between service workers and laborers, was described in Chapter 3. Equation 3.1 provides the formula for testing the significance of the difference between two groups designated by binary-coded dummy variables. The reader can use the results reported in Table 3.1 to verify that the two procedures produce identical t values and that the contrast and its standard error are identical to the estimated difference in means and the standard error of the difference defined by Equation 3.1.

REFERENCES

ALBA, R. D. (1988) "Interpreting the parameters of log-linear models," pp. 258-287 in J. S. Long (ed.) Common Problems/Proper Solutions: Avoiding Error in Quantitative Research. Newbury Park, CA: Sage.
ALDRICH, J. H., and NELSON, F. D. (1984) Linear Probability, Logit, and Probit Models. Sage University Paper series on Quantitative Applications in the Social Sciences, 07-045. Beverly Hills, CA: Sage.
ALLISON, P. D. (1984) Event History Analysis: Regression for Longitudinal Event Data. Sage University Paper series on Quantitative Applications in the Social Sciences, 07-046. Beverly Hills, CA: Sage.
AMEMIYA, T. (1986) Advanced Econometrics. Cambridge, MA: Harvard University Press.
BARTLETT, M. S. (1937) "Properties of sufficiency and statistical tests." Proceedings of the Royal Society of London 160 (Series A).
BERRY, W. D., and FELDMAN, S. (1985) Multiple Regression in Practice. Sage University Paper series on Quantitative Applications in the Social Sciences, 07-050. Beverly Hills, CA: Sage.
BOHRNSTEDT, G., and KNOKE, D. (1982) Statistics for Social Data Analysis. Itasca, IL: F. E. Peacock.
CHEN, C. (1984) "The structural stability of the market model after the Three Mile Island accident." Journal of Economics and Business 36: 133-140.
CHOW, G. C. (1960) "Tests of equality between sets of coefficients in two linear regressions." Econometrica 28: 591-605.
CLOGG, C. C., and GOODMAN, L. A. (1984) "Latent structure analysis of a set of multidimensional contingency tables." Journal of the American Statistical Association 79: 762-771.
CLOGG, C. C., and GOODMAN, L. A. (1985) "Simultaneous latent structure analysis in several groups," pp. 81-110 in N. Tuma (ed.) Sociological Methodology. San Francisco: Jossey-Bass.

COHEN, J., and COHEN, P. (1983) Applied Multiple Regression (2nd ed.). Hillsdale, NJ: Lawrence Erlbaum.

CONOVER, W. J., JOHNSON, M. E., and JOHNSON, M. M. (1981) "A comparative study of tests for homogeneity of variances with applications to the Outer Continental Shelf bidding data." Technometrics 23: 351-361.

DARLINGTON, R. B. (1990) Regression and Linear Models. New York: McGraw-Hill.

DUNN, O. J. (1961) "Multiple comparisons among means." Journal of the American Statistical Association 56: 52-64.

GLEJSER, H. (1969) "A new test for homoscedasticity." Journal of the American Statistical Association 64: 316-323.

GOLDFELD, S. M., and QUANDT, R. E. (1972) Nonlinear Methods in Econometrics. Amsterdam: North-Holland.

GOLDFELD, S. M., and QUANDT, R. E. (1978) "Asymptotic tests for the constancy of regressions in the heteroscedastic case." Research Memorandum No. 229, Econometric Research Program, Princeton University.

GOODMAN, L. A. (1978) Analyzing Qualitative/Categorical Data. Cambridge, MA: Abt Associates.

GUJARATI, D. N. (1970) "Use of dummy variables in testing for equality of sets of coefficients in two linear regressions: A note." American Statistician (February).

GUJARATI, D. N. (1988) Basic Econometrics (2nd ed.). New York: McGraw-Hill.

HABERMAN, S. J. (1978) Analysis of Qualitative Data, Vol. 1: Introductory Topics. New York: Academic Press.

HABERMAN, S. J. (1979) Analysis of Qualitative Data, Vol. 2. New York: Academic Press.

HALVORSEN, R., and PALMQUIST, R. (1980) "Interpretation of dummy variables in semilogarithmic equations." American Economic Review 70: 474-475.

IDLER, E. L., and KASL, S. (1991) "Health perceptions and survival: Do global evaluations of health status really predict mortality?" Journal of Gerontology 46(2): S55-65.

JACCARD, J., TURRISI, R., and WAN, C. K. (1990) Interaction Effects in Multiple Regression. Sage University Paper series on Quantitative Applications in the Social Sciences, 07-072. Newbury Park, CA: Sage.

JOHNSTON, J. (1984) Econometric Methods (3rd ed.). New York: McGraw-Hill.

KENDALL, M. G., and STUART, A. (1979) The Advanced Theory of Statistics, Vol. 2 (4th ed.). New York: Charles Griffin.

KMENTA, J. (1986) Elements of Econometrics (2nd ed.). New York: Macmillan.

LEVENE, H. (1960) "Robust tests for equality of variances," pp. 278-292 in I. Olkin (ed.) Contributions to Probability and Statistics. Stanford, CA: Stanford University Press.

LEWIS-BECK, M. S. (1980) Applied Regression: An Introduction. Sage University Paper series on Quantitative Applications in the Social Sciences, 07-022. Beverly Hills, CA: Sage.

LONG, J. S., and MIETHE, T. D. (1988) "The statistical comparison of groups," pp. 108-131 in J. S. Long (ed.) Common Problems/Proper Solutions: Avoiding Error in Quantitative Research. Newbury Park, CA: Sage.

MADDALA, G. S. (1983) Limited-Dependent and Qualitative Variables in Econometrics. Cambridge: Cambridge University Press.

MADDALA, G. S. (1992) Introduction to Econometrics (2nd ed.). New York: Macmillan.

MILLER, R. G., Jr. (1966) Simultaneous Statistical Inference. New York: McGraw-Hill.

MUTHEN, B. (1984) "A general structural equation model with dichotomous, ordered categorical, and continuous latent variable indicators." Psychometrics 46: 115-132.

RYAN, T. A. (1960) "Significance tests for multiple comparisons of proportions, variances, and other statistics." Psychological Bulletin 57: 318-328.

SCHROEDER, L. D., SJOQUIST, P. L., and STEPHAN, P. E. (1986) Understanding Regression Analysis: An Introductory Guide. Sage University Paper series on Quantitative Applications in the Social Sciences, 07-057. Beverly Hills, CA: Sage.

SHOCKEY, J. W. (1988) "Latent-class analysis: An introduction to discrete data models with unobserved variables," pp. 288-315 in J. S. Long (ed.) Common Problems/Proper Solutions: Avoiding Error in Quantitative Research. Newbury Park, CA: Sage.

SUITS, D. (1983) "Dummy variables: Mechanics v. interpretation." Review of Economics and Statistics 66: 177-180.

WELCH, B. L. (1938) "The significance of the difference between two means when the population variances are unequal." Biometrika 29: 350-362.

WINSHIP, C., and MARE, R. D. (1983) "Structural equations and path analysis for discrete data." American Journal of Sociology 89: 54-110.

WINSHIP, C., and MARE, R. D. (1984) "Regression models with ordinal variables." American Sociological Review 49: 512-525.

ABOUT THE AUTHOR

MELISSA A. HARDY is Professor, Department of Sociology, and Director of Research, Institute on Aging, at Florida State University in Tallahassee. She received her Ph.D. in 1980 from Indiana University, Bloomington. Her current research includes studies of labor force participation among older men and women, recent changes in retirement policies and practices, social mobility, and the feminization of poverty. She has published articles in numerous journals, including *American Sociological Review, Sociology of Education, Health and Social Behavior, Demography,* and *Research on Aging.*